Even If It Ain't Broke Yet, Do Fix It

Enhancing Effectiveness Through Military Change

Even If It Ain't Broke Yet, Do Fix It

Enhancing Effectiveness Through Military Change

Vivek Chadha

idsa
INSTITUTE FOR DEFENCE STUDIES & ANALYSES
NEW DELHI

PENTAGON PRESS

Even If It Ain't Broke Yet, Do Fix It: Enhancing Effectiveness Through Military Change
Vivek Chadha

First Published in 2016

ISBN 978-81-8274-919-1

Published by
PENTAGON PRESS
206, Peacock Lane, Shahpur Jat,
New Delhi-110049
Phones: 011-64706243, 26491568
Telefax: 011-26490600
email: rajan@pentagonpress.in
website: www.pentagonpress.in

In association with
Institute for Defence Studies and Analyses
No. 1, Development Enclave,
New Delhi-110010
Phone: +91-11-26717983
Website: www.idsa.in

Printed at Aegean Offset Printers, Greater Noida, U.P.

Contents

PART II
MILITARY CHANGE IN COUNTERINSURGENCY

PART III
ANALYSING MILITARY CHANGE

ACKNOWLEDGEMENTS

I am grateful to Dr. Arvind Gupta, former Director General, IDSA and currently Deputy NSA, for guiding the project during its initiation and Shri Jayant Prasad, Director General, IDSA, for supporting it through its culmination. I am also thankful to Brig. Rumel Dahiya, Deputy Director General, IDSA, for his sage advice and facilitation of roundtables and fellow paper presentations, which provided valuable inputs for the project.

The project benefitted immensely through the inputs by discussants, both external and internal, including Lt. Gen. Satish Nambiar, Lt. Gen. Mukesh Sabharwal, Lt. Gen. D.S. Hooda, Maj. Gen. Umong Sethi, Brig. Gurmeet Kanwal, Brig. Rahul Bhonsle, Gp. Capt. Naval Jagota, Gp. Capt. Ajey Lele and Col. Vijai Singh Rana. I would also like to acknowledge the support of the Military and Internal Security Centres at IDSA, for their valuable inputs, as well as the external reviewers who constructively critiqued the Fellow Paper and the final manuscript of the book diligently.

I would like to acknowledge the Paper titled *The Indian Army Adapting to Change: The Case of Counter-Insurgency*, as part of a larger project undertaken by the Centre for Asian Security Studies at the Norwegian Institute for Defence Studies, Oslo, that led to the publication of the book, *Security, Strategy and Military Change in the 21st Century: Cross-Regional Perspectives.* This Paper initiated the thought process on the subject and was developed into a section on counterinsurgency warfare in this book, duly enlarged both in context and scope. The inputs from the exceptional participants at the conference at Oslo and the support from Jo Inge Bekkevold, who guided the project, helped initiate the process.

The relatively nascent subject led to hours of deliberations and arguments with my colleagues at IDSA and in particular Col. Rajeev Agarwal and Cdr. Abhijit Singh. Their inputs were very useful in helping shape the study. The tireless support of Vivek Kaushik during the publication of the book, Neha Kohli for publication of a paper related to the same subject in the *Journal of Defence Studies,* the library staff, forever eager and helpful, Rajan Arya, the publisher at Pentagon Press, whose positive support remains steadfast, the efficient Virender Negi who formatted the manuscript, and Nidhi Pant, a thorough editor, deserve special mention.

I would like to thank the IDSA administrative staff for their continuing support through the conduct of events and publication of papers that led to this book. Finally, I would like to thank my family for their encouragement of not only this project, but also my endeavours in the field of research.

Vivek Chadha

List of Tables and Charts

Introduction

Military change as a subject for both academics and practitioners remains a perplexing challenge. A number of attempts have been made to explain its definition, connotations, drivers, pathways, impact and conditions that facilitate its manifestation and implementation. This has not only been an obsessive concept for military analysts, but also management gurus who have made an endeavour to explain it in terms of corporate entities. Tomes have been written – arguments and counter-arguments continue to rage across published papers. However, the challenge of explaining the phenomenon remains open to interpretation and individual understanding.

Thus, this Volume not only attempts to outline the definitive understanding of the subject, but also reinforces that the process is complex and tends to be influenced by a number of different factors and conditions which may be peculiar to a country or region. It is therefore unlikely to be explained through a singular framework. A large number of theoretical constructs are needed to explain it accurately in parts and under certain circumstances. Particularly, there seems to be no single, easy explanation for understanding military change with army as a basis, given its peculiar conditions of employment across the spectrum of conflict.

The complexity of military change has primarily been commented upon from the perspective of conventional, or state-on-state conflicts, in the past. However, exceptions to this are highlighted through case studies presented in this Volume, which further complicate its understanding. For example, the emphasis on *major shifts* and *innovations* in the conventional domain related to external wars tends to get diluted in counterinsurgency (CI) operations, and *operational factors* at the tactical level tend to gain significance instead. In effect, change management in CI operations becomes more challenging than conventional threats for a number of reasons, which in turn impact the quality and pace of change:

One, a conventional threat to a country receives undiluted and comprehensive focus from every state element including the armed forces, consequently increasing the state's chances of overcoming the threat. At the same time, though a number of factors may still prevent this process from succeeding; however, the determination of the state apparatus is rarely the reason for the same. On the other hand, in the case of CI operations, depending upon the importance given to a particular threat or region, the focus and efforts of individual states vary. If the threat is considered merely an irritant that can be managed, change management is unlikely to receive the support it needs. For example, in the past, localised military changes were attempted to neutralise threats like improvised explosive devices (IEDs); however, it took more than a decade to bring a more formalised solution to the problem with the induction of Casspir vehicles.

Two, conventional threats remain the primary focus of armies, especially in the case of the Indian Army, given the country's unresolved borders. This limits the time and attention that is afforded to counterinsurgency, which is seen and is designated as a secondary responsibility. This leads to far less time and resources being applied to its management, adversely affecting change management in CI operations.

Three, a number of examples of change management can be seen in conventional warfare, wherein armies were able to pre-empt their adversary through forward-looking strategic thought, doctrines and application of technology. This, however, has not been the case in CI operations, where the army has played catch-up and remained behind the learning curve. This is partly influenced by the army adapting to each conflict on receipt of orders for induction. There are no specific designated formations for this task. Given the geographical proximity of units, the task falls upon those in the vicinity of the conflict. Thus, besides generic training and preparation for CI threats, which is a part of curriculum in courses of instruction, the army cannot prepare for such eventualities, as well as the situation may demand. This is especially relevant for time-consuming activities like intelligence build up.

Thus, a contradiction arises which is often difficult to reconcile. In the past, the differences in courses of action for conventional vis-à-vis CI threats have led authors to deal with these vastly different operational domains in distinct air-tight compartments. Moreover, it presents a bigger challenge to a military planner, be it in uniform or as part of civilian defence planning staff. Therefore, change management cannot be isolated for different operational responsibilities till the time it is meant to be undertaken by the same army. Unlike in the past, recent years have clearly indicated that armies across the world are equipped to take up responsibilities for operations other than war. This sub-conventional domain, including CI operations, has been a major operational responsibility for a number of armies. Thus, any future changes that are envisaged must not only cater to the primary raison d'être of armies, which is fighting conventional armies, but also non-traditional security threats, especially CI and counterterrorism.

There has been an ongoing argument in relation to how change manifests. Is it driven by a top-down process, led by the senior military leadership with support from the government? Or, does it emerge on the basis of bottom-up feedback? As the book reveals, both these processes remain relevant under different environments. Moreover, from the perspective of implementing policy options for effective change management in the future, it remains imperative to keep an ear to the ground. Particularly, certain important factors like the changing nature of the operational environment and impact of technology must be understood better so that future leaders are suitably equipped to deal with the emergent challenges. Very often limitations related to military leadership are brushed aside with the argument that an army which has acquitted itself well over the decades must obviously be "doing the right thing" vis-à-vis its professional conduct. However, for an organisation which is as large and traditional as the Indian Army, not only is it challenging to bring about major changes, it takes an equally long time for its effectiveness to be affected by the inability to change. Therefore, limitations if any, may well manifest through a process which may not be immediately discernible. It is often for this reason that the organisational or strategic culture of an army develops over a protracted period of time, before it cements into a perceptible trait.

The evolution of these changes, which have come to best illustrate the army's organisational and strategic culture, is reflected in a number of spheres. While some of these directly impact operations, others have a lasting influence on the conduct of the officer cadre, and therefore, the rank and file of the organisation. The foundation of the army's conduct after independence, was laid on the principles of professionalism, secularism and remaining apolitical. Brigadier Khanduri has expounded on Field Marshal Cariappa's views on these subjects: Cariappa "enforced discipline and strictness to keep politics out of officers' messes, their schools of instruction, the men's barracks and billets".[1] The same was emphasised by General T.N. Raina, who withstood all pressures to allow any linkage with political dispensations during the emergency in 1975,[2] and this was also reinforced by most succeeding senior leaders of the army over the years. General J.J. Singh described the three pillars of the army as: professionalism, secularism and being apolitical.[3] These principles continue to guide generations of officers in the army and have stood the test of time.

The case studies related to CI operations clearly illustrate that the political and military guidance was in favour of adopting a policy which viewed insurgents as misguided fellow-countrymen, who should ideally be brought back into the national mainstream. This was accompanied by the Indian Army adopting the principle of minimum force, one of the very few armies in the world which refuses to utilise heavy calibre weapons, artillery and helicopter gunships against these violent movements. Similarly, India's policy of non-interference in neighbouring countries and emphasis on employing armed forces primarily for the defence of the country are vital facets of India's military culture.

The role and contribution of the armed forces in the evolution of the country's strategic culture has often been a subject of debate. This has in part been affected by the limited interest and specialisation on military issues amongst the political elite and the wider community. However, there are only a few officers who have made a significant contribution to shaping strategic thought in the country. Amongst the foremost is General K. Sundarji, who had a profound impact on the country's nuclear policy. He was also instrumental, along with others like General Krishna Rao, in initiating the strategic underpinnings of the conduct of modern warfare in India, at least from the army's perspective. Similarly, Lt Gen Satish Nambiar has helped guide understandingof UN peacekeeping and India's role as part of the global effort over the years.

However, these outstanding examples represent a small minority rather than the larger majority. The is reinforced by case studies as well as a survey of officers included in this book which suggest that the role and ability of the military elite in influencing the debate on the larger issue of national security has remained limited. This is a result of the inability of the existing system, both within and outside the army to groom leaders suitably for national and strategic responsibilities. While limited exposure to strategic issues in the army constrains the growth of leaders, more importantly, the existing policy which affords a marginal role to senior officers within the national security apparatus is the major factor responsible. It is also clearly evident that the same officers who are able to display sterling qualities of leadership on the tactical battlefield, and excel under fire, are unable to graduate to the strategic domain and provide similar direction and guidance, as a result of systemic weaknesses in the defence and national security architecture, which does not afford them opportunities for assuming the desired role.

The governing structure's failure to incorporate military leadership at the highest levels of decision-making has resulted in the flow of multilayered and filtered military advice reaching the decision-making authorities. It also leads to the military elite remaining equally constrained in their understanding of national issues by virtue of this disconnect with the decision-making structures at the national level. This condition is neither conducive nor desirable for implementing military change.

At the functional level, the inability to suitably equip the officer cadre relates to the structure and conduct of imparting professional military education (PME) and providing a suitable professional environment. It emerges that this environment is not conducive for the growth of military leaders, especially those holding senior positions in the army. While the challenges of PME relate to the inability to imbibe creativity and open thinking, the failure of strategic foresight emerges from the inability to understand the larger issues of national security. The focus of PME is so deeply embedded in tactical issues that the foundation of strategic building blocks remains weak amongst junior and middle rung officers. This is further accentuated by institutional structures which are unable to help bridge the gap between tactical and strategic understanding of issues. These limitations adversely affect the ability to initiate and implement military change since gaps in understanding of strategic issues will invariably affect this process.

This is also affected adversely by the lack of specialisation amongst officers, continued emphasis on ceremonials, formation-level commitments with an accompanying zero error syndrome. As the survey suggests, such an environment is unlikely to facilitate creative thinking, which is the essence for change management.

One of the critical components of political support for military change is adequacy of financial outlay for major organisational changes. The two case studies analysed as part of major organisational changes in the conventional domain suggest that the government had met the financial requirements for these changes, as is evident from the hike in defence expenditure during the period succeeding the 1962 War and 1975 report on restructuring of the army. This point needs greater emphasis in the present context, since it is likely to have an impact on present and future structural reorganisations. In this regard, two factors deserve to be put into perspective:

First, unlike in the past when the government allowed a major increase in defence budget to cater for restructuring, the same has not been witnessed in case of the ongoing transformation of the army. The cost of raising an additional corps by 2018-19 has been estimated at 64,678 crore.[4] In the absence of these funds, the army could be forced to partially readjust resources from within to cater for this increase. This is likely to further lower existing deficiencies and war wastage reserves, which are essential to maintain a battle-worthy army.

Second, major organisational restructuring has led to an increase in the size of the army in the past. The Indian Army, which increased its numbers from 5,50,000 to 8,25,000 after the 1962 War, further increased its numbers thereafter to a strength of approximately 1.16 million at present.

In the present context, the raising of 17 Corps will lead to an additional increase in the strength of the army. As a result of this sustained increase in numbers, the army is being forced to allocate a larger percentage of its budget to revenue rather than capital expenditure, thereby affecting modernisation. The demand-allocation gap in defence outlay has increased from 9 per cent in 2009-10 to 26 per cent in 2014-15, and the revenue budget is approximately 80 per cent of the 2015-16 army budget allocation.[5] In the near future, these numbers will come under even greater strain with the government having to allocate additional funds for meeting the demands of the seventh pay commission which will be effective from 01 January, 2016. This places a question mark on the ability of the government to support the nature of organisational changes that have been planned. It also requires the army to review its policy of employing increasing numbers in the quest for ensuring security, wherein quite clearly, this is likely to come at a cost of its modernisation efforts. If the fighting edge of the army has to be maintained, then the administrative tail must be reduced to better balance the military budget.

Keeping in view these realities, in 2015, the Prime Minister stated in no uncertain terms the anomaly of size and modernisation:

> Modernisation and expansion of forces at the same time is a difficult and unnecessary goal. We need forces that are agile, mobile and driven by technology, not just human valour ... We have been slow to reform the structures of the our Armed Forces. We should shorten the tooth-to-tail ratio.[6]

He went on to outline the role of military leaders in this regard:

> We need military commanders who not only lead brilliantly in the field, but are also thought leaders who guide our forces and security systems into the future.[7]

Layout of Book

The book has been structured keeping in mind the reality of a broad spectrum of operations undertaken by the Indian Army. Despite using the term military change, which is part of the academic lexicon on the subject of change management in the operational and strategic sphere, the scope of this book is limited to the army.

The first chapter includes a literature survey with an aim of outlining existing writings on the subject of military change. This helps to put into perspective varying points of view and frameworks by authors who have written on the subject over a period of time. It also provides a backdrop for evaluating succeeding case studies and analysing the process of change management though prevailing perspectives.

Chapter 1 is followed by Part I: Conventional Threats, a section, including Chapters 2, 3 and 4, on military change in relation to the conventional environment which is usually associated with state-on-state wars. The section takes up case studies under the purview of organisational and strategic changes in the Indian environment. This provides the groundwork for conclusions to be drawn in relation to military change and an analysis of drivers, shapers and contributing conditions which facilitate the process.

Similarly, Part II, which includes Chapters 5, 6, 7, and 8, discusses sub-conventional warfare, with special emphasis on CI operations. The section briefly elaborates upon 27 case studies under the strategic, organisational and operational domains. This description provides the basis for a better understanding of the nature of change, its direction, drivers, form and impact. In doing so, the section also outlines important factors which can facilitate military change in the CI operations, while commenting on the quality, pace and nature of change that has been witnessed in the Indian environment over the years.

In Part III, Analysing Military Change, individual assessment of the two aforementioned sections is amalgamated for a detailed comment on its relation and relevance to change in the corporate sector, which too wrestles with similar procedural challenges. A co-relation of organisational change provides the necessary basis for attempting a comparison of changes in the Indian Army with theoretical frameworks analysed in the Chapter 1. This provides an opportunity to note areas of convergence from past studies, as also differences that do not necessarily apply in the Indian context.

Finally, the last chapter attempts to encapsulate some of the major takeaways at the governmental level and validates the conclusions of the project through a survey of both serving and retired officers of the Indian Army in different service brackets. This helps put the conclusions into perspective and highlight issues, which best reflect the areas of weaknesses as well as strengths of the army in relation to its ability to adapt to change. This is especially relevant when seen as an attempt to outline existing challenges and possible options to future change management.

NOTES

1. Brig. C. B. Khanduri, *Field Marshal K.M. Cariappa: His Life and Times*, Lancer Publishers, New Delhi, 1995, p. 235.
2. Ibid., p. 236.
3. Gen. J. J. Singh, *A Soldier's General: An Autobiography*, Harper Collins, New Delhi, 2012, p. 199.
4. Rajat Pandit, "Army Chief Reviews Mountain Strike Corps", *The Times of India*, May 8, 2014, at http://timesofindia.indiatimes.com/india/Army-chief-reviews-mountain-strike-corps/articleshow/34795843.cms (Accessed April 04, 2015).
5. Laxman K. Behera, "India's Defence Budget 2015-16", Institute for Defence Studies and Analyses, March 02, 2015, http://www.idsa.in/issuebrief/IndiasDefenceBudget2015-16_lkbehera_020315.html, accessed March 27, 2015.
6. Narendra Modi, "PM Chairs Combined Commanders' Conference on Board INS Vikramaditya at Sea", PM India, December 15, 2015, at http://pmindia.gov.in/en/news_updates/pm-chairs-combined-commanders-conference-on-board-ins-vikramaditya-at-sea/?comment=disable (Accessed March 22, 2016).
7. Ibid.

1

Existing Theoretical Frameworks

Militaries, given their strict hierarchical setup and tight bureaucratic norms, often display a somewhat predictable disinclination for change. A series of interactions with the officers of the Indian Army during the course of interviews for this book reinforced this assertion. The officers reacted with surprising predictability to uniformly brush aside any semblance of success with change management. Nevertheless, change has and will continue to take place. The challenge is to discern its direction and destination.

The debate is equally vibrant with regard to the very concept of military change, its constituents, drivers, pathways and even the level at which it takes place. There is also a degree of overlap between the concept of military change and innovation. Often some of these terms are used interchangeably. This is especially the case with early writings on the subject, which related change to innovation. These issues often tend to get diffused depending on the perspective of an author, which could be primarily academic in nature, thereby focussing on relating it to an existing or new theoretical framework. For others, its real-life application gains significance, especially when seen from the position of a practitioner. The understanding is also linked to the spectrum of operations viewed by an author, while analysing the concept of change. As literature on the subject suggests, assessment of state-on-state or conventional threats provides a very different perspective when compared to sub-conventional operations like counterinsurgency and counterterrorism. Military change at times tends to indicate contradictory linkages and derivates in either case, even though these relate to the same armed forces employed at different stages of their timeline.

This raises some questions regarding the very concept of change, its constituents, pathways and factors which help bring it about, especially when seen from a cross-platform perspective that includes both conventional and sub-conventional changes and trends. In order to provide an overview of existing literature on these issues and how it describes and explains military change as well as its constituents and contributors, this chapter attempts a literature survey of the subject. This will hopefully provide the basis for evaluating the succeeding case studies, as also analyse their relevance. It also provides an understanding of a subject, which despite being an intrinsic process to all militaries, tends to either get brushed aside as a result of an innate acceptance of the inability to change or taken for granted, being an integral part of day-to-day life.

What is Military Change?

There is an interchangeable usage of the terms innovation and military change as seen in the common pool of literature reviewed to describe it. The only purpose of continuing with this practice in this chapter, despite the book focussing on military change, is to capture the essence of existing literature on the subject[1] – particularly in light of authors linking major changes to innovation in several cases.

Grissom provides a good summation of the explanations that have been used for describing innovation. He divides past studies into four schools of research for explaining innovation, namely the civil-military, inter-service, intra-service and cultural models. The civil-military model suggests that the nature of relationship between the civilian leadership and the military is critical for militaries to innovate.[2] Grissom further relates the work of Kimberly Zisk on the Soviet doctrinal development and Deborah Avant on the US and British performance in counterinsurgency (CI) operations to the same model.[3] The inter-service model emphasises on the importance of competition between different services amongst the armed forces, which compete to retain control over resources, which forces them to innovate. The intra-service model suggests that it is the competition within services that leads to innovation. Here, he relates

Stephen Peter Rosen's work on innovation as the basis for the model.[4] Finally, the cultural model reinforces that culture is the major reason for innovation, wherein he cites Farrell's work as the primary source for this prognosis.[5]

In contrast, a more recent volume, *Security Strategy and Military Change in the 21st Century*, studies a cross-section of literature from Asia, Europe and the US.[6] It concludes that a single theoretical perspective does not adequately explain the nature of changes that have been and are being experienced by militaries the world over. The authors instead attempt to employ a combined theoretical perspective emerging from the neorealist, organisational and cultural theories to explain the changes.[7] The neorealist school suggests that strategic competition and a state's external environment is responsible for its choices. The insecurity that emanates as a result leads to military change. Organisational theory relates to the internal dynamics of the political and military establishments. This therefore encompasses aspects like the inter-agency, intra-agency or civil military models. A more detailed assessment of the work of individual authors is required to explain some of these models and their relation to military change.

Military change was mainstreamed by Barry Posen in his book, *The Sources of Military Doctrine: France, Britain and Germany Between the World Wars*.[8] However, Posen did not deal specifically with change, though, he did delve upon the subject of innovation and doctrinal evolution. He employed the organisational as well as balance of power theory to elaborate upon and examine doctrines.

Stephen Peter Rosen, while acknowledging Posen's seminal work, looks at military innovation under three categories to include peacetime, wartime and technological change. He defines military change in the context of peacetime and wartime as "change in one of the primary combat arms of a service in the way it fights or alternatively, as a creation of a new combat arm".[9] He further states,

> A major innovation involves a change in the concepts of operation of that combat arm, that is, the ideas governing the ways it uses its forces to win a campaign, as opposed to a tactical innovation, which is a change in the way individual weapons are applied to the target and environment in battle. A major change also involves a change in the relation of that combat arm to other combat arms and a downgrading

or abandoning of older concepts of operations and possibly a formerly dominant weapon.[10]

Rosen stresses that changes in formal doctrine of a military organisation may not alter the functioning of the organisation, and hence, cannot be considered as part of military change. Moreover, he elaborates on the concept of technological innovation with a caveat, as major innovations could take place without 'behavioural changes' in the organisation. He also relates change to the creation or co-relation of combat arms in battle, thereby bringing about major innovation. It could also imply a simultaneous change in strategic or doctrinal considerations.

Theo Farrell and Terry Terriff, in their book, *The Sources of Military Change: Culture, Politics and Technology*, provide a different perspective of military change. They do not discount the importance of military doctrine as a medium of bringing about change; however, the authors highlight the limitations therein: Some armies lack a doctrinal tradition; the doctrinal interpretation varies depending on the different national contexts; the military organisation may not change despite changes in doctrine; and finally, the doctrine may end up merely as a political statement rather than a strategic guideline.

Farrell and Terriff also question the limitations of Rosen's definition, since it does not include changes in the objectives of military operations. In particular, Farrell refers to a broader definition which identifies "change in the goals, actual strategies, and/or structure of a military organisation" as military change.[11] For example, in the period between the two world wars, the US Marine Corps changed its organisational goals by shifting its role – from light infantry to amphibious warfare. A change in strategy was adopted during the same period from a battleship-based naval strategy to aircraft carriers. Furthermore, such shifts witness organisational changes, for example, by replacing battle fleets with carrier task forces. Evidently, it leads to the desirability of major changes with a substantial impact on the functioning of a force. The authors consciously exclude from this definition minor tactical and technological changes which do not have an impact on organisational strategies and structures.

Adam Grissom defines military adaptation, as "a change in operational praxis that produces a significant increase in military effectiveness, as measured by battlefield results".[12] Grissom, thus, finds that three key factors are common with most literature on the subject. This includes a major impact on how a military fights in war; it should be significant; and finally, lead to greater military effectiveness.

Military change often tends to get associated with adaptation in relation to external state on state conflicts. However, the world in the recent past has witnessed an evolving nature of threats which have manifested at the sub-conventional level. This has forced the US and its allies to adapt, often in a hurry, to the nature of existing challenges, for example, those faced in Iraq and Afghanistan. A lot has been written about the experience of the US and its allies in these conflicts. However, literature on change in the sub-conventional domain remains limited. Theo Farrell, Frans Osinga and James A. Russell's *Military Adaptation in Afghanistan* analyses the subject in detail. Farrell, in the introductory chapter, defines military adaptation as: "Change to strategy, force generation, and/or change to military plans and operations, undertaken in response to operational challenges and campaign pressures."[13] The definition has been included based on the theme and context of the book, and therefore, its applicability beyond such scenarios may not necessarily be valid. Force generation includes "force levels, equipment, training, and doctrine". Unlike the context of most other works referred to, in this chapter, the impact of sub-conventional operations becomes apparent, since its applicability includes both strategic and operational levels of war.

Further, according to Farrell and Terriff, innovation is not the same as military change, as it is at times considered. They see military innovation as one of the outcomes of military change, simultaneously identifying it as major or minor. They go on to highlight three pathways to military change, namely innovation, adaptation and emulation, described as follows:

> Innovation involves developing new military technologies, tactics, strategies, and structures. Adaptation involves adjusting existing military means and methods. Adaptation can, and often does, lead to innovation when multiple adjustments over time gradually lead to the evolution of new means and methods. Last emulation involves importing new tools and ways of war though imitation of other militaries organisations. It is only when these new military means and methods result in new organisational goals, strategies, and structures that innovation, adaptation, and emulation lead to major military change.[14]

Interestingly, many years prior to this formulation, Clausewitz had suggested his set of pathways. He felt that armies change as a result of historical examples, personal battlefield experience and experience of other armies. He indicated that militaries will change based on their being witness to successful innovations by others, which suggests the desire to change something which subsequent research contradicts.[15]

Why Do Militaries Change?

If militaries are averse to change, then what forces them to implement it? The debate over the sources of military change is characterised by different views on the subject, just as the literature review suggests.

Posen employs organisational and balance of power theory, in an attempt to understand doctrines and their evolution. He uses organisational theory to amplify on military "behaviour" and "preferences".[16] He suggests that modern states designate functions for respective bureaucracies, and adds that non-soldiers will find it difficult to evaluate military needs and will remain dependent on soldiers for advice. On the other hand, military organisations will resist civilian control. In the case of Britain, France and Germany between the world wars, only civilians could bring about change in doctrines by overcoming this limitation. Posen reinforces the factor of resistance to change amongst militaries, given the comfort levels achieved by the senior leadership based on old doctrines.[17] He further attributes resistance to change to the hierarchical nature of the organisation, which impedes the flow of ideas. He also suggests that the refusal to innovate on part of militaries creates a gap between grand strategies and their follow-up military strategies. Inter-service competition further often leads to poor implementation of such strategies, given the pursuance of their individual interests. Services tend to fight for their share and often when strategies have the potential to upset status quo, these are opposed as a result. This, according to Posen, leads to circumstances wherein services merely pay lip service to joint doctrines and these remain a compilation of the individual doctrines of services. Civilian intervention is seen as the only means of breaking this condition.

Posen further uses balance of power theory to analyse the employment of an offensive-defensive or deterrence-oriented doctrine as also its correlation with innovation.[18] He cites the example of Germany to suggest its employment of offensive doctrine during the Second World War, as an example of passing the war costs to the adversary by fighting in its territory. It was intended to safeguard the industrial infrastructure of the country and prevent Hitler's legitimacy from being questioned. In addition, Hitler waged a "preventive" war in a multipolar environment, which facilitated the exploitation of windows of opportunity, through an offensive doctrine. Further, political isolation facilitated use of offensive measures as an adjunct to diplomacy. According to Posen, deterrence is employed when military capabilities are limited and countries in a coalition prefer to fight based on a defensive doctrine. Under these conditions, he finds that civilian leaders are likely to have closer integration with the military and the military is likely to innovate better when states are isolated.[19] He gives the example of Germany prior to the Second World War and Israel in the more recent past to validate his argument.

Barry Posen explains the concept of innovation, as a form of large change and attributes it to three factors. The first is as a result of failure; second, due to pressure from without; and third, when organisations wish to expand.[20] On the basis of empirical evidence, he cites two sources of innovation.[21] First, military organisations tend to learn from wars fought by their client states. He gives the example of the 1973 Arab-Israel War and its impact on both the US and erstwhile USSR. Second, armies learn even better from their own use of technology in wars. Posen cites examples of the evolution of the Prussian doctrine for use of rail road between 1850 and 1870 to reinforce this proposition. He however adds a caveat to this by highlighting that the senior leadership often remains separated from the reality of the front lines, which brings distance to changes taking place. This can lead to failure to innovate based upon battlefield experience. The inability of generals to adapt to trench warfare witnessed during the American civil war and subsequently during the First World War is an example of this limitation. Reinforcing the influence of change from without, he gives examples of Britain, France and Germany, wherein, change at the doctrinal level was brought about by civilian intervention.

Posen reinforces the importance of civilian leadership to bring about comprehensive change. He feels that periods of peace are likely to allow militaries to remain unchecked in their pursuit of military doctrines. This can lead to contradictions between military and political objectives and worse, military doctrines being contrarian to the grand strategy of a country.[22] While acknowledging the challenges of military change, he concludes that change can best be brought about by civilian intervention supported by military 'mavericks' who are willing to move against conventional wisdom and yet provide the necessary expertise for helping initiate change.

The interference or influence of "statesmen" in matters military is highlighted in the case of Britain during the Second World War. The adoption of a deterrent/defensive doctrine based on the international environment, led to a change in the Royal Air Force's bombing doctrine. Civilians became the fulcrum of change through the adoption of a defensive doctrine, despite resistance of the military. The independence of the military hierarchy for a decade and the prevalence of organisational theory during this period ultimately failed to give results, and the balance of power theory better explains the British doctrine finally adopted during the period.

The French example quoted by Posen interestingly highlights the decision of the political leaders, despite achieving victory during the First World War, to force its military to give up the offensive doctrines in favour of defensive. This was done to cut possible costs, and despite the innovative creation of the Maginot Line, stagnation of doctrines did not support changes witnessed in the period preceding the Second World War.

Rosen analyses peacetime and wartime change separately. While discussing peacetime change, he argues that defeat in war is "neither necessary nor sufficient to produce innovation". He goes on to suggest that militaries are unlikely to innovate in peacetime, given their inherent characteristics. Military innovation, according to Rosen, "must be the result of civilian intervention". While disagreeing with the role of military mavericks, he suggests that peacetime change can only be brought about by those who wield power in an organisation. Mavericks do not have such power, as they are more of outsiders. Conversely, he contends that "respected senior military officers" within the system are best suited to bring about innovation, given their position to influence strategy for innovation.

Rosen analysing wartime military change suggests that the limitations placed on time during a war impinge upon the ability to bring about change. He says that "wartime innovation will be limited in its impact where it does occur at all, because the time necessary to complete all these tasks is likely to be long relative to the length of the war".[23] This is especially related to the limitations placed on the availability of intelligence leading to a "fog of war". Further, Rosen indicates that it will be easier for a centralised and hierarchical organisation to innovate, given their ability to better understand conditions and circumstances, unless a decentralised organisation needs to innovate independently, without a simultaneous need to bring about changes in the larger organisation. He suggests that technological innovation is not merely a result of "technology push", "demand pull" or a qualitative arms race with the adversary or even a cost-benefit analysis. He visualises its development as a means of managing uncertainty.[24]

Theo Farrell and Terry Terriff see change emanating from cultural norms, politics and strategy and finally technology.[25] They define cultural norms as "intersubjective beliefs about the social and natural world that define actors, their situations, and the possibility of action".[26] This then creates the environment both for individuals as well as organisations to operate in. It also assists them through guidelines, which have come to be accepted over a period of time. Since these guidelines impact behaviour, they also become important determinants for change management. The abhorrence for nuclear weapons is rooted in their usage during the Second World War. Similarly, Japan's policies on issues of non-proliferation are deeply influenced by it. India's policy of anti-colonialism and apartheid were also reflected in its sufferings at the hands of an imperial power. Similarly, military behaviour and change also reflects the cultural ethos of a country.

Farrell and Terriff take the example of events linked with the Cold War to illustrate the importance of strategy and politics as a source of military change. War termination forced a rethink of the prevailing strategic environment, which in turn forced a change in operational planning. The strategic environment also forced a change, which required the US military to prepare for peacekeeping and peace enforcement missions. This Avant and Labovic feel was a result of political intervention.[27]

The importance of technology to drive military change has also received attention of authors in the past, since the advent of new technology leads to its incorporation, which brings about a revolutionary change in the conduct of operations. Here Farrell and Terriff present two major schools of thought, wherein the first suggests that advancement in technology will lead to better or more complex weapon systems, thereby bringing about change. The second school suggests that the social debate which centres around a design determines the nature of final product, since there is more than one way of designing and creating a product. However, the salience of technology as a source of military change is reinforced nonetheless.

Organisational culture has been defined in many ways over a period of time and often in relation to its contextual reference. Lundy and Cowling give a simple and easy to understand definition which sees organisational culture as "the way we do things around here".[28] Martins and Terblanche define it as, "the deeply seated (often subconscious) values and beliefs shared by personnel in an organisation".[29] A more specific assessment of organisational culture in the case of militaries suggests a similar context. Peter H. Wilson argues that "military culture is a specific form of institutional culture and that viewing armies from this perspective offers new insight into how they functioned and the nature of their interaction with state and society". He further defines it as, "The values, norms, and assumptions that guide human action. Culture enables choices to be made by predisposing people to interpret situations in a limited number of ways."[30]

An army's strategic culture is closely linked with its organisational culture. Amongst the sources of strategic culture are the defence organisations of a country.[31] An understanding of the attributes and constituents of strategic culture will further provide an understanding regarding its co-relation with the organisational culture of an army. With reference to nuclear issues, Snyder defines strategic culture as "a set of general beliefs, attitudes, and behavioural patterns with regard to nuclear strategy that has achieved a state of semi-permanence that places them on the level of "cultural" rather than mere policy". Johnston defines it as the "ideational milieu that limits behavioural choices," from which "one could derive specific predictions about strategic choice". Rosen's definition describes it as "beliefs and assumptions that frame ... choices about international military behaviour, particularly those concerning decisions to go to war, preferences for offensive, expansionist or defensive modes of warfare, and levels of wartime casualties that would be acceptable".[32] Previously, strategic culture has also been identified as one of the drivers for military change. The external influences on the strategic culture of a country or an army includes factors like threats. However, threats cannot be divested from the potential or the actual use of force, which in many ways is a simple way of understanding strategic culture. A country's strategic culture can be assessed by the manner and circumstances which lead to the employment of force over a period of time in a nation's history. For Colin Gray, a first generation theorist dealing with strategy, there is a clear linkage between strategic culture and strategic behaviour.[33] While this relates to a country, its impact is equally profound on the army, which is the instrument of utilisation of force against both internal and external threats.

There is an interesting contrast which is presented in this regard, as indicated by Dima Adamsky, who suggests that cultural aspects became a more important factor in military innovation than merely technology.[34] Accordingly, the author suggests that Russian interest in technology was related to defence transformations, whereas for the US, it was its tactical application. The Israelis applied it as a force multiplier, without changing the structure of their forces. These cultures led the Russian senior hierarchy, which took the lead in intellectual development of ideas to develop concepts for future wars, at times ahead of the availability of technology. In contrast, the US, as a result of its bottom-up approach did not allow for preparation in advance for the impending changes. Finally, the Israeli emphasis on non-traditional threats led them to neglect military theory and doctrine. Further, Adamsky suggests the importance of "norm entrepreneurs" in their role of not only changing the discourse but also framing the necessary policies for bringing about military change. The role of these leaders from important positions of power or influence is also reinforced in accordance with Rosen's understanding of change management.

Going further on the aspect of military culture, Williamson Murray provides both a broad overview of the importance of military culture in armies across the world, and thereafter, a more focussed assessment of the US defence forces.[35] He cites examples from the German culture which reflects in their excellence at tactics and disdain for logistics during the world wars. The German culture of troop leadership and emphasis on professional military education (PME) after the First World War, largely through the efforts of Hans von Seeckt, was reflected in the excellence of commanders like Rommel. Similarly, he notes that the Italian disdain for attention to detail, reflects in their planning for war during the same period. The French inability to face the impracticality of their plans after the First World War, stemmed from their failure to study the past and learn from it. In contrast, the Americans established 20 separate study groups after the War to analyse its lessons, which formed a part of their Field Service Regulation in 1923, providing the necessary doctrinal underpinnings.[36] This according to Murray has witnessed a shift with an over-reliance on technology and its envisaged power and influence on the modern battlefield: "This summer's war game at Newport indicated that some in the navy believe that 'the great data base in the sky' will provide U.S. commanders with absolute knowledge of everything that happens in an enemy nation in the next war."[37] A lot of these limitations were attributed to a sense of "anti-intellectualism" and remaining "ahistorical". This in turn was related to challenges of PME in the armed forces. With the exception of the marines, who had attempted to upgrade their educational system, Murray notes, "Not surprisingly, the navy does not have a professional reading list, the air force's list is remarkable for its shortness and superficiality, the army's list remains largely unavailable to its officer corps."[38] He also remarks on the worrying trend of the forces not being able to debate issues, which remains the basis for critiquing ideas and concepts in a progressive organisation.

In the foreword to John Nagl's seminal book, *Learning to Eat Soup with a Knife*, the former US Chief of Army Staff, General Peter J. Schoomarker wrote,

> The organisational culture of the U.S. Army predisposed to fight a conventional enemy that fought using conventional tactics, overpowered innovative ideas from within the Army and from outside it. As a result the U.S. Army was not as effective at learning as it should have been, and its failures in Vietnam had grave implications for both the Army and the nation.[39]

In contrast, the British Army was seen as more adaptive, again primarily as a result of their adaptive organisational culture that had gained from a series of irregular warfare experiences.[40] Nagl suggests that not only did the US Army fail to adapt during the conflict, but also learnt the wrong lessons. The hierarchy preferred to adopt a narrow understanding of reasons that led to the defeat.[41] This was also accompanied by the rejection of CI operations as a realistic and possible involvement of US forces in future conflicts, further reinforcing their emphasis on conventional conflicts.

Nagl finds this is best illustrated through doctrines and standard operating procedures adopted by the army. This according to him is often the product of institutional memory, which tends to emerge in the form of doctrinal writings and changes thereupon, and these doctrines are "trailing indicators of institutional learning". However, if an organisation fails to take note of lessons learnt, even if doctrines emerge, these are likely to be based on a weak foundation, thereby resulting in its failure.

Nagl's work is focussed on CI operations. It is possibly for this reason that he rightly focusses more on lessons from the combat zone, which is often an intimate reflection of limitations in existing thinking and the need for change. Despite this limitation, his emphasis and focus on organisational and strategic culture remains relevant even for conventional operations.

Elaborating upon the learning processes, though with specific relation to CI operations, Nagl emphasises the need for an organisation to accept its inability to achieve its objectives under existing conditions. This according to him best emerges from the ranks of junior officers who are closest to the reality of conflict. Thus, innovation and changes emerge from the field and are best accompanied by the force of doctrinal top-down execution of orders, especially given the evolving circumstances in operations.[42] Nagl underlines the importance of leadership as an important factor in driving innovation, through the selection and vision of leaders like Briggs and Templer during the Malaya campaign. Their understanding of the importance of "politics in unconventional warfare", was the sign of deep understanding of the challenge at hand. In contrast, the US experience displayed a contrasting organisational culture, which did not pay heed to bottom-up feedback and reliance on attrition to defeat the adversary.[43]

Furthermore, Nagl relates change management to organisational theory. He attributes the success of the British Army, in its endeavour to adapt conventional tactics to the sub-conventional methods in Malaya to "several complete iterations of the organisational learning cycle".[44] This is further linked to the traditional flexibility of thought and action of the British and their army's organisational culture. He attributes it to the class composition of the British society and relaxation of rank structure. Interestingly, Nagl highlights the British employment of a CI doctrine merely as a guideline rather than a sacrosanct manual for operating in CI operations. He quotes General Frank Kitson: "Doctrine is prepared in order that the Army should have some basis for training and equipping itself. You certainly don't fight based on your doctrine! If you actually do fight based on your doctrine you're letting yourself in for disaster."[45] In contrast, according to Nagl, the US Army failed to adapt after the conflict in Vietnam, given its conventional orientation to operations. The US Army further saw the victory of the First Gulf War as vindication of its new doctrines, failing to assimilate the reality of future wars.

Janine Davidson analyses military change from the perspective of learning processes within armies. She feels that it is this learning process that has a greater impact on military change, when compared to organisational culture and external political intervention. This according to her as a result of internal institutional structures and processes can "prevent, promote or permit military change through learning".[46] She disagrees with analysts like John Nagl, who attribute the success or failure of innovation to organisational culture. She feels that the years after the Cold War failed to "capture and disseminate" the lessons, which in contrast was done better as a result of structures and procedures designed to act as a counterweight to entrenched organisational culture.[47] This emphasises the importance and need for an army which is structured to make best use of operational lessons as part of the teaching and learning structures and processes. The Americans did a better job of this immediately in the aftermath of the Gulf War and further into Afghanistan, according to Davidson.

The challenges of PME and building the intellectual capital of the army has been addressed by Lt Gen. Syed Ata Hasnain in the Indian context. This essential capability is critical for creative thinking, innovation and ultimately facilitating military change. As a result, according to Lt Gen. Hasnain, "Intellectualism is linked to very few names among our senior officer cadre."[48] The importance of PME is reinforced by Lt Gen. Prakash Menon, who calls it the "bedrock of military effectiveness that progressively hones and shapes the proficiencies of military professionals to shoulder responsibilities that are commensurate with rank and appointment".[49]

Moreover, K Subrahmanyam highlights the lack of training to equip officers at senior levels. He feels that the senior ranks of the armed forces in India are constrained by "lack of opportunities for senior officers to equip themselves for higher posts, which involve long range, future-oriented planning".[50] This clearly includes their ability to conduct strategic planning, organisational restructuring and operational orientation in line with future challenges.

The existing framework provided by authors like Rosen as well as Ferrell and Terriff for research on military change is biased towards conventional operations, as is most other work analysed separately on the subject.[51] The limitations of this body of literature on military innovation and change become evident in the context of a sub-conventional environment, characterised by operations against insurgents and terrorists.

Further, Farrell, Osinga and Russell identify the drivers in the context of a sub-conventional threat, as it exists in Afghanistan. Quite clearly, this witnessed a distinct differentiation in the nature of challenges faced by the US led forces. The primary driver for military adaptation remained operational challenges.[52] This was relevant as threat was seen more of a relevant driver in conventional circumstances. Technology is yet again a factor, which continued to influence military adaptation in a region like Afghanistan. The authors identify domestic politics, alliance politics, strategic culture and civil-military relations as the other factors influencing the ability to adapt in such conditions. Evidently, alliance politics is a factor peculiar to regions like Afghanistan, where a coalition of nations need to coordinate and cooperative towards the achievement of common and yet at times conflicting ends.

Rajesh Rajagopalan's *Fighting Like a Guerrilla: The Indian Army and Counterinsurgency* is amongst the few books that explain Indian Army's attempt to adapt to change in CI operations. Rajagopalan argues that the "Indian Army has been able to adapt to counterinsurgency to a limited extent, and that the primary limitation has been the strong conventional war bias in the doctrine".[53] While this argument does find credence in the initial stages of the army's involvement in CI operations, however, over a period of time and as the Sub Conventional Doctrine of the Indian Army[54] reinforces, these influences have in large measure been replaced by a distinct CI approach, with variations relevant to different areas of operations.

This chapter provides a limited overview of existing literature. Despite this constraint, varying perspectives on military change and its derivates are quite apparent. The review raises issues like the implication of military change, its meaning, causes and pathways. Further, this book attempts to address these in succeeding chapters through case studies which will highlight some of these aspects in the Indian context. In doing so, an attempt has been made to derive conclusions, which can help contextualise the relevance of these aspects thereafter.

NOTES

1. Farrell and Terriff disagree with the interchangeable usage of the two terms and clearly relate innovation as a pathway to military change.
2. Adam Grissom, "The Future of Military Innovation Studies", *The Journal of Strategic Studies*, 26 (5), October 2006, p. 908.
3. Kimberly Marten Zisk, *Engaging the Enemy: Organization Theory and Soviet Military Innovation, 1955-1991*, Princeton University Press, New Jersey, 1991; Deborah D. Avant, *Political Institutions and Military Change: Lessons from Peripheral Wars*, Cornell University Press, Ithaca, 1994.
4. Stephen Peter Rosen, *Winning the Next War: Innovation and the Modern Military*, Cornell University Press, Ithaca, 1991.
5. Theo Farrell and Terry Terriff (eds.), *The Sources of Military Change: Culture, Politics, Technology*, Lynne Rienner Publishers, Boulder, 2002.
6. Jo Inge Bekkevold, Ian Bowers and Michael Raska (eds.), *Security Strategy and Military Change in the 21st Century: Cross-Regional Perspectives*, Routledge, New York, 2015.
7. Ibid., p. 266.
8. Barry Posen, *The Sources of Military Doctrine: France, Britain and Germany Between the World Wars*, Cornell University Press, Ithaca, 1984.
9. Stephen Peter Rosen, No. 4, p. 7.
10. Ibid., pp. 7-8.
11. Theo Farrell and Terry Terriff, No. 5, p. 5.
12. Adam Grissom, No. 2, p. 907.
13. Theo Farrell, Frans Osinga and James A. Russell (eds.), *Military Adaptation in Afghanistan*, Stanford University Press, Stanford, 2013, p. 2.
14. Theo Farrell and Terry Terriff (eds.), No. 5, p. 6.
15. Janine Davidson, *Lifting the Fog of Peace: How American's Learned to Fight Modern War*, University of Michigan Press, Ann Arbor, 2010, p. 10.
16. Barry Posen, No. 8, p. 222.

17. Ibid., p. 224.
18. Ibid., pp. 229-230.
19. Ibid., p. 232.
20. Ibid., p. 47.
21. Ibid., p. 56.
22. Ibid., p. 241.
23. Stephen Peter Rosen, No. 4, p. 38.
24. Ibid., p. 52.
25. Theo Farrell and Terry Terriff (eds.), No. 5, p. 6.
26. Ibid., p. 7.
27. Deborah D. Avant and James H. Lebovic, *U.S. Military Responses to Post-Cold War Missions*, in Theo Farrell and Terry Terriff (eds.), No. 5, p. 139.
28. O. Lundy and L. Cowling, quoted in E.C. Martins and F. Terblanche, "Building Organisational Culture that Stimulates Creativity and Innovation", *European Journal of Innovation Management*, 6 (1), 2003, p. 65.
29. Ibid. (E. C. Martins and F. Terblanche).
30. Peter H. Wilson, "Defining Military Culture", *The Journal of Military History*, 72 (1), January 2008, p. 14.
31. John Baylis, James J. Wirtz and Colin S. Gray, *Strategy in the Contemporary World*, Oxford University Press, Oxford, 2013, p. 81.
32. Ibid., p. 80.
33. Colin Gray, "Strategic Culture as Context: The First Generation of Theory Strikes Back", *Review of International Studies*, 25 (1), January 1999, p. 50.
34. Dima Adamsky, *The Culture of Military Innovation: The Impact of Cultural Factors on the Revolution in Military Affairs in Russia, the US, and Israel*, Stanford University Press, Stanford, 2010, pp. 132-134.
35. Williamson Murray, "Does Military Culture Matter?" *Orbis*, 43 (1), Winter 1999, pp. 134-151.
36. Ibid., p. 141.
37. Ibid., p. 146. (The period refers to the mid-nineties)
38. Ibid., p. 147.
39. General Peter J. Schoomaker, Foreword to John A. Nagl, *Learning to Eat Soup with a Knife: Counterinsurgency Lessons from Malaya and Vietnam*, University of Chicago Press, Chicago, 2005, p. ix.
40. Ibid. (John A. Nagl), p. xii.
41. Ibid., pp. 206-207.
42. Ibid., 192-195.
43. Ibid., p. 198.
44. Ibid., p. 192.
45. Ibid., p. 204.
46. Janine Davidson, No. 15, p. 192.
47. Ibid.
48. Lt Gen. (Retd) Syed Ata Hasnain, "Is it Worth Discussing Military Intellectualism?", *South Asia Defence and Strategic Review*, July 24, 2014, at http://www.defstrat.com/exec/frmArticleDetails.aspx?DID=479 (Accessed February 15, 2016).
49. Lt Gen. Prakash Menon, "Military Education in India: Missing the Forest for the Trees", *Journal of Defence Studies*, 9 (4), October-December 2015, p. 52.
50. K. Subrahmanyam, "Structure and Personnel Policy of the Armed Forces", in K.

Subrahmanyam and Arthur Monteiro, *Shedding Shibboleths: India's Evolving Strategic Outlook*, Wordsmiths, Delhi, 2005, p. 64.

51. The select literature on the subject analysed includes: Barry Posen, No. 8; Adam Grissom, No. 2; Deborah D. Avant and James H. Lebovic, No. 27.
52. Theo Farrell, Frans Osinga and James A. Russell (eds.), No. 13, p. 3.
53. See Rajesh Rajagopalan, *Fighting Like a Guerrilla: The Indian Army and Counterinsurgency*, Routledge, New Delhi, 2008, p. 29.
54. See *Doctrine for Sub Conventional Operations*, Integrated Headquarters of Ministry of Defence (Army), Headquarters Army Training Command, Shimla, December 2006.

PART I

Conventional Threats

MILITARY CHANGE IN THE INDIAN ARMY: CASE OF EXTERNAL THREATS

Change, military or corporate, is considered a challenge, given the inherent resistance of organisations and their desire to remain in their comfort zone. Stephen Peter Rosen suggests, "Almost everything we know about large bureaucracies suggests not only that they are hard to change, but that they are *designed not to change*."[1] Past experience suggests that more often than not, military bureaucracies fit this description, as their tradition-bound nature creates an inherent distaste for change.[2] Ironically, the very nature of modern combat is based on the ability to Observe, Orient, Decide and Act, which is referred to as the OODA loop. Thus arises a contradiction, wherein the fundamental nature of bureaucracies, including military bureaucracies, is to resist change, even as the critical requirement for militaries to succeed is based on the ability to successfully manage change.

If the only constant in life is change, then military change should be a continuum.[3] However, the theory of organisational behaviour suggests just the reverse.[4] This brings into focus the *nature of change*, as a critical factor of this perceptional anomaly. One finds that while militaries as a routine go about adaptation as either an operational requirement, or a result of constraints, it is the transition of major change, characterised by innovations, that remains a challenge. For example, the Indian Army is known for its ability to successfully operate in a variety of roles from disaster relief to CI operations and peacekeeping missions to conducting international sporting events. Even while fulfilling its primary role of defending the country against external threats, battlefield adaptation is the norm rather than the exception. However, much like other armies, which adapt well but find it challenging to successfully undertake major changes, the Indian Army also faces a similar dilemma.

In the present context of the army, this dilemma becomes relevant all the more so. One, it comes at a time when attempts are underway to transform the army by including changes at the strategic and organisational level, which are aimed at improving efficiencies and overall combat effectiveness. General V.K. Singh, the former Chief of Army Staff, stated that these changes would "reorganise, restructure and relocate" formations, in order to achieve enhanced agility and lethality.[5] Two, the changes are likely to be planned and executed under conditions which will demand greater effectiveness and efficiency, even as budgets available for capital expenditure are likely to come under strain. Three, unlike the previous cases of major change, the present context has to cater for a full spectrum capability which could diffuse the focus of the army from its primary responsibility against external threats. Despite these peculiar conditions, there is little doubt that the success of the ongoing transformation can benefit from the army's past experiences of change management. These experiences both successful and not so successful can not only help the learning process on the basis of the previous results achieved, but more importantly, provide insight into the processes followed as well as their weaknesses that limited the ultimate gains.

The chapters in this section (Part I: Conventional Threats) will assess military change from two perspectives that include change in the organisational structure and military strategy of the army. Since these are two of the principle domains in which military change manifests itself, the case studies analysed provide a reasonable understanding of the process.

NOTES

1. Stephen Peter Rosen, *Winning the Next War: Innovation and Modern Military*, Cornell University Press, Ithaca, 1991, p. 2.
2. Theo Farrell and Terry Terriff (eds.), *The Sources of Military Change: Culture, Politics, Technology*, Lynne Rienner Publishers, Boulder, 2002, p. 4.
3. The quote of change being the only constant in life is attributed to the ancient Greek philosopher, Heraclitus.
4. Janine Davidson, *Lifting the Fog of Peace: How Americans Learned to Fight Modern War*, University of Michigan Press, Ann Arbor, 2010, at https://www.press.umich.edu/pdf/9780472117352-ch1.pdf, pp 10-11 (Accessed April 29, 2015).
5. Nitin Gokhale, "India's Doctrinal Shift", *The Diplomat*, January 25, 2011, at http://thediplomat.com/2011/01/indias-doctrinal-shift/?allpages=yes.

2

An Assessment of Organisational Change

The Indian Army has post-independence attempted to undertake military change on several occasions. However, the number of instances that reflect major shifts in terms of attempts at innovation remain limited. Amongst these, the changes after the 1962 India-China War and post-1975 K.V. Krishna Rao committee recommendations remain the most significant. In addition to these, the army also undertook organisational changes after the 1999 Kargil conflict and Operation Parakram in 2001, besides changes related to the ongoing transformation.

The implementation of military change after the 1962 War and 1975 recommendations fulfil the broad parameters for organisational military change better than some other more recent attempts at change management by the army. For example, the changes after Operation Parakram were limited to realignment of boundaries of formations opposite Pakistan, by raising the additional corps headquarters, as well as command headquarters. However, this did not result in accretion of force levels and was more an exercise in reallocation of resources to enable greater "synergy" and "create more reserves and enhance the inherent offensive defence capability in the theatre".[1] A similar exercise had earlier been undertaken with the raising of the corps headquarters, based on the lessons learnt after the 1999 Kargil conflict. This assisted in improving command and control and surveillance capabilities.[2] The most recent structural change began with the raising of a corps oriented towards mountain warfare, with its principle focus on the border with China. However, given the evolutionary stage of this formation, an assessment could suggest misleading conclusions, especially in light of the Defence Minister's remarks on the possibility of cutting down the size of the corps.[3]

The change related to the raising of Rashtriya Rifles (RR) has also been excluded, despite this being a significant organisational shift, as it primarily focussed on the sub-conventional threat in Jammu and Kashmir (J&K) and along the Line of Control (LoC) with Pakistan. (This discussion forms a part of the next section, Part II – Military Change in Counterinsurgency that deals with changes in the counterinsurgency environment in India.)

In contrast, the changes post-1962 led to an increase in the army's size by almost 33 per cent. It also saw the raising of divisions, which were tailored to the needs of mountain warfare, and command headquarters, which directly influenced the ability to employ these newly raised formations. Moreover, not only did the post-1975 changes transform the army's organisational structure, but the resultant innovations had a lasting impact on its strategic thought, which continued to guide subsequent adaptations. Ideally, the case study dealing with post-1975 changes should have benefitted from access to the Krishna Rao Committee report. However, in its absence, as a result of it being classified, Gen. Krishna Rao's book, *Prepare or Perish: A Study of National Security*,[4] provided the basis as well as the broad parameters for the changes envisaged. These, along with the actual changes over the next two decades, give a clear direction of changes undertaken, which is instructive.

Changes Post 1962 Sino-Indian War

India's defeat against China in the 1962 War led to a series of organisational changes in the Indian Army. These changes took place at all levels, impacting the foot soldier as well as the overall structure of the army. This section provides an overview of the changes to assess the nature of structural reforms undertaken.

Three major structural changes took place, which impacted the size and structure of the army. *First,* based on the recommendations of the army, the government sanctioned the increase in its size, from 5,50,00 to 8,25,000.[5] *Second*, a large percentage of this force accretion included the raising of divisions, tailored in terms of their organisation, equipment profile and training for mountain warfare. Of the six divisions initially raised, four were new mountain divisions and one plains division was converted to a mountain division.[6] There is a strong possibility that the final figure of the army's size was influenced by the scale of US assistance that was being negotiated and finally agreed upon. This is indicated by US discussions on the subject in 1963, wherein a figure of 8,00,000 seemed to be acceptable rather than the Indian demand for 1.4 million army personnel.[7] *Third*, a new command headquarters, the Central Command, was setup in May 1963 in Lucknow, with a focus on the threat from China.[8]

Three important directorates were also reorganised within Army Headquarters for greater efficiency. The Weapons and Equipment Directorate was shifted from Master General of Ordnance to General Staff Branch, as was Military Survey from Engineer-in-Chief Branch. There was also an attempt to strengthen the Military Intelligence Branch, in view of past limitations.[9]

The army also undertook the raising of Scout battalions for deployment in vicinity of the border with China in the Northern and Central Sectors. The troops for these battalions were recruited from hill tribes in local areas and their role was similar to that of the Assam Rifles in Northeast India along the border.[10]

In addition, the army majorly upgraded its training capacity to cater to the increase in intake of officers and personnel below officer rank alike. Under the emergency commission, 9,000 officers were granted commission in the period from November 1962 to October 1964. Officers training academies were established at Pune and Chennai in January 1963. Innovative schemes were introduced to recruit officers to the medical and engineering arms, including antedate seniority to cater to their length of service prior to commission, reservation of jobs in government service after release of emergency commission officers and university entry schemes. These measures saw the training capacity expand from approximately 5,700 to 40,000 over a short period of time.[11] Given the inexperience of fighting in mountains, there was additional stress on mountain and high-altitude warfare.[12]

The change in the organisation of the army would have been incomplete without the accompanying induction of weapons and equipment. Some of the major changes in this regard included the sanction to induct the 7.62 mm self-loading rifle, instead of the Second World War-vintage .303. Short- and medium-range mortars were introduced to improve the fire power of battalions. Mountain guns with high trajectory firing capability were inducted. A decision was also taken to purchase both medium and light tanks. The army had 38 per cent, 68 per cent and 15 per cent pre-1948 vehicles to include 3 tons, 1 ton and jeeps, respectively.[13] A decision was taken to modernise this fleet through the induction of Tata Mercedes Benz (3 tons), Dodge (1 ton) and Willys jeeps. An ordnance factory was established at Avadi to meet the additional clothing and parachutes needs. In order to cater to the needs of buildings to house additional formations and training establishments, 1,883 works projects were sanctioned under emergency provisions.[14]

The shortcomings noticed in the intelligence systems, supply of equipment, staff work procedures, physical fitness of troops and higher direction of war were also noted, and changes were initiated. A Directorate of Combat Development was established under the General Staff Branch to review tactical concepts, development of organisations and materials in light of new tactical concepts and conduct of trials in formations and experimental formations.[15]

The changes were accompanied by equitable allocation of financial resources to undertake the envisaged measures. This is evident from the steep rise in defence expenditure immediately after the 1962 War (see Table 1).

Table 1: India's Defence Spending: 1962-1967 (as a percentage of GDP[16])

Year	1962-63	1963-64	1964-65	1965-66	1966-67
Def Exp/GDP	2.56	3.84	3.25	3.38	3.07

Source: Air Cmde Jasjit Singh, *India's Defence Spending: Assessing Future Needs*[17]

The organisational changes were planned and suggested by the army, with influence of British and US defence advisers in terms of the equipping profile, since equipment for the mountain divisions was being provided by the US. This influence stemmed from their desire to ensure that the equipment would be used only against China and not Pakistan and the transfers would be just adequate for India to defend itself. This was evident during then US Defence Secretary, Robert McNamara's visit to India when he expressed disappointment to then Defence Minister, Y.B. Chavan, because of the unjustifiably long list of demands by the Indian Defence forces to US representatives.[18] This was reinforced by declassified US papers, which suggested an unrealistic Indian plan of increasing force levels to a 1.4 million army with an annual budget of $ 1.8 million and an aid package of $ 1.4 billion.[19]

The military defeat against China led to an attempt at streamlining implementation of various changes within the government, and also found support therein.[20] Y.B. Chavan, the new defence minister, who replaced Krishna Menon after the 1962 War, realised that a number of organisational changes were being undertaken without a clear assessment of the country's strategic goals.[21] This lack of clarity forced Chavan to order a strategic assessment of India's military needs in order to structure the process of induction of military hardware, as well as raising of new formations. This included an assessment based on inputs from the Ministry of External Affairs (MEA) and intelligence agencies.[22]

The confusion and lack of clarity in the process being followed prior to this assessment is reinforced by Maj. Gen. D.K. Palit, who was the Director Military Operations (DMO) during the 1962 War and was instrumental in preparing the suggested blueprint for the organisational restructuring of the army. According to him, the initial requirement was to equip 50 divisions.[23] However, this was revised to 25, 21, 16 and back to 21 divisions over a period of time, with little assessment of application of force.[24] He further alleges a lack of strategic understanding in the rationale for decision-making by the senior leadership of the army, especially with reference to its expansion plans.[25] Palit's assessment of the situation was echoed to an extent by General Taylor, Chairman of the US Joint Chiefs of Staff, who wrote:

> In the case of the military programme, there are as yet no agreed time-phased levels of force goals, no plan for the allocation of available or anticipated resources to the needs of the three services, and no determination of the kind and extent of foreign aid needed to augment domestic resources.[26]

Even as organisational changes were progressively implemented, these were constrained by service specific planning. Palit offers a similar critique with respect to creating the new command headquarters. He notes that these actions were based on spur-of-the-moment decisions on the part of General Chaudhuri, without analysing the implications of co-locating them with the Air Force, or practicality of operational effectiveness thereby affecting joint planning and operations.[27]

Reforms Post K.V. Krishna Rao Report

The government appointed an expert panel in 1975 to undertake, probably for the first time, a long-term perspective plan for the army.[28] The committee was headed by Lt Gen. (later Gen.) K.V. Krishna Rao, with Maj. Gens. M.L. Chibber and K. Sunderji as members and Brig. A.J.M. Homji as secretary.[29] It was mandated to present a perspective till the year 2000. The committee was required to evaluate national security threats, propose a strategy against it, visualise the future battlefield, determine the size of the army and suggest an incremental build-up of forces.[30] Wide-ranging discussions were carried out with various agencies, including the Indian Space Research Organisation and Planning Commission. This ensured that the committee was able to collate a cross section of views prior to making its recommendations. These changes aimed at improving the teeth to tail ratio of the army, making it organisationally lean, even as it pursued modernisation.

This report followed up on the limited mechanisation of the army that had begun in 1969 with the induction of TOPAZ and SKOT armoured personnel carriers. As a result of the recommendations of the report, this received an impetus with the raising of the Mechanised Infantry Regiment on April 2, 1979, equipped with Infantry Combat Vehicles (Boyevaya Mashina Pekhoty; or BMPs).[31] The real impact of these recommendations was felt when Sundarji took over as the Chief of Army Staff in 1986. By the end of his tenure, 23 mechanised battalions had been raised, most equipped with BMP-2, thereby utilising the best technology available. More importantly, he provided the strategic moorings for employment of mechanised forces.[32] His vision laid the foundation for the transition of a Second World War army to a modern force, with reliance on fast-paced operations and tenets of manoeuvre battle. This was facilitated by the raising of the Army Aviation Corps in 1986, induction of 155 mm Bofors guns, re-designating an infantry division as an air assault division and raising of Reorganised Army Plains Infantry Divisions (RAPIDs), with an enhanced component of armour and mechanised infantry.[33]

These innovations, as in the case of the post-1962 organisational changes, were initiated by officers from the army. However, there is strong evidence that Gen. Sundarji was able to push one of the fastest induction process in the army, based on his personal rapport with the Minister of State of Defence, Arun Singh, and Prime Minister, Rajiv Gandhi. According to Inderjit Badhwar and Dilip Bob,

> At no other time, except possibly the period just before the Indo-Pak conflict of 1971, has the Indian military and political leadership been so closely associated. Delhi's bold initiatives in power projections, its new diplomatic aggressiveness, its euphoric confidence is obviously correlated to the new rapport that Sundarji had established with the political high command.[34]

The impact of Sundarji's drive, strategic vision and close working relationship with the political elite created substantial changes in the army's organisational structure. Besides the acquisition of assets, it laid the foundation for mobile warfare and simultaneously propelled a change in the thinking of the army's leadership. This was based on a change in the army's doctrine as well. It shifted from defensive deterrence to "deterrence by punishment" during the eighties, bordering on compellence.[35] The shift reflected signs of a changing strategic culture in the army, which was injected by offensive thinking and a more robust approach to potential adversaries. (This will be analysed in greater detail in a subsequent chapter.)

The changes were also accompanied by the willingness of the government to provide greater allocation of financial resources to facilitate the process. Defence expenditure during this period rose sharply to finance the structural changes (see Table 2), as seen from the period wherein most weapon platform inductions took place. However, while the initial changes benefitted from generous financial outlays, subsequent years yet again witnessed a cut, which adversely impacted implementation of complementary changes like ensuring matching mobility of support echelons, thereby stalling the follow-up action.

Table 2: India's Defence Spending: 1982-1990 (as a percentage of GDP)

Year	1982-83	1983-84	1984-85	1985-86	1986-87	1987-88	1988-89	1989-90
Def Exp/GDP	3.04	3.04	2.88	3.05	3.58	3.59	3.37	3.17

Source: Air Cmde Jasjit Singh, *India's Defence Spending: Assessing Future Needs*[36]

While the committee benefitted from wide-ranging interactions with other government agencies, it was saddled with an inherent limitation. The government in its bid to assess long-term defence preparedness constituted different committees for all the services.[37] Inherent in this initiative lay seeds of service-specific modernisation, rather than a joint effort, which could have led to greater synergy and unity of action.

NOTES

1. Gen. J.J. Singh, *A Soldier's General: An Autobiography*, Harper Collins, New Delhi, 2012, p. 193.
2. See Gen. V.P. Malik, *Kargil: From Surprise to Reckoning*, Harper Collins, New Delhi, 2006, pp. 354-355.
3. "Mountain Strike Corps Size to be Cut", *Deccan Herald*, April 14, 2015, at http://www.deccanherald.com/content/471696/mountain-strike-corps-size-cut.html (Accessed April 24, 2015).
4. Gen. K.V. Krishna Rao, *Prepare or Perish: A Study of National Security*, Lancer Publishers, New Delhi, 1991.
5. *Annual Report 1964-65*, Ministry of Defence, Government of India, p. 17; K. Subrahmanyam, "The Ghosts of 1962", in K. Subrahmanyam and Arthur Monteiro, *Shedding Shibboleths: India's Evolving Strategic Outlook*, Wordsmiths, New Delhi, 2005, p. 323.
6. After this initial raising, the total number of mountain divisions increased to 10. Government of India,
7. Bromley Smith, "Document 293, Summary of Record of the 514th Meeting of the National Security Council", *Foreign Relations of the United States, 1961-1963, Volume XIX, South Asia*, Office of the Historian, Bureau of Public Affairs, United States Department of State, Washington, May 09, 1963, at http://history.state.gov/historicaldocuments/frus1961-63v19/d293 (Accessed March 22, 2015).
8. A.L. Venkateswaran, *Defence Organisation in India*, Publications Division, Ministry of Information and Broadcasting, Government of India, 1967, pp. 146-147.
9. See *Annual Report 1963-64*, No. 6, p. 22.
10. See *Annual Report 1963-64*, No. 6, p. 23.
11. A.L. Venkateswaran, No. 8, pp. 205-208.
12. See *Annual Report 1963-64*, No. 6, p. 21.
13. 3-ton and 1-ton vehicles denote their load carriage capacity.
14. See *Annual Report 1963-64*, No. 6. pp. 36-39.
15. See *Annual Report 1963-64*, No. 6, p. 22.
16. GDP refers to Gross domestic product.

17. Air Cmde Jasjit Singh, *India's Defence Spending: Assessing Future Needs*, Knowledge World, New Delhi, 2000, p. 23.
18. Personal interaction with R.D. Pradhan, former Principal Secretary to Y. B. Chavan, March 22, 2015.
19. R.W. Komer, "Document 283, Memorandum for the Record", *Foreign Relations of the United States, 1961-1963, Volume XIX, South Asia,* Office of the Historian, Bureau of Public Affairs, United States Department of State, Washington, April 25, 1963, at http://history.state.gov/historicaldocuments/frus1961-63v19/d283 (Accessed March 22, 2015).
20. See Jawaharlal Nehru, "April 14, 1962", in G Parthasarthi (ed.), *Letters to Chief Ministers: 1947-1964, Vol 5 1958-1964*, Oxford University Press, Delhi, 1989, p. 585. Air Commodore Jasjit Singh confirms the doubling of the defence expenditure after the War to meet the modernisation needs, in *The Icon: Marshal of the Air Arjan Singh, DFC,* K W Publishers, New Delhi, 2009, p. 137.
21. R.D. Pradhan, *Debacle to Resurgence: Y.B. Chavan*, Defence Minister (1962-66), Atlantic Publishers, New Delhi, 2013, pp. 210-211.
22. Personal interaction with R.D. Pradhan, No. 18.
23. Maj. Gen. D.K. Palit, *War in the High Himalayas*, Lancer International, New Delhi, 1991, p. 380.
24. Ibid., p. 403.
25. Ibid., p. 403, 407-409.
26. Maxwell D. Taylor, "Document 348, Memorandum from the Chairman of the Joint Chiefs of Staff (Taylor), to Secretary of Defense McNamara", *Foreign Relations of the United States, 1961-1963, Volume XIX, South Asia*, Office of the Historian, Bureau of Public Affairs, United States Department of State, Washington, December 23, 1963, at http://history.state.gov/historicaldocuments/frus1961-63v19/d348 (Accessed March 24, 2015).
27. Maj. Gen. D.K. Palit, No. 23, p. 372.
28. Gen. K.V. Krishna Rao, No. 4, p. 400.
29. Maj. Gen. Ian Cardozo, *The Indian Army: A Brief History*, United Service Institution of India, New Delhi, 2005, p. 159.
30. Ibid.
31. "Evolution of Mechanised Infantry", Indian Army, Official Indian Army Web Portal, at http://indianarmy.nic.in/Site/FormTemplete/frmTempSimple.aspx?MnId=dBeaewznZhW5edwodwN7Dg==&ParentID=bEltdB/PwPcT8w3ACPSSYQ==.
32. The army pamphlets on combat group employment were published for the first time in the early eighties and followed by armoured division in battle in the early nineties.
33. See Inderjit Badhwar and Dilip Bob, "General K. Sundarji: Disputed Legacy", *Indian Today*, May 15, 1988, at http://indiatoday.intoday.in/story/general-sundarji-leaves-behind-a-legacy-most-fiercely-disputed-in-the-history-of-the-army/1/329290.html. The division did not achieve the status it was designated for and subsequently converted to a RAPID.
34. Ibid.
35. Ali Ahmed, *India's Doctrine Puzzle: Limiting War in South Asia*, Routledge, New Delhi, 2014, pp 41-45.
36. Air Cmde Jasjit Singh, No. 17.
37. See G.M. Hiranandani, *Transition to Eminence: The Indian Navy 1976-1990*, Lancer Publishers, New Delhi, 2005, pp. 158-159.

3

STRATEGIC MILITARY CHANGE

Chapter 2 analysed organisational or structural changes in the army in the aftermath of the 1962 Sino-Indian War, as well as those based on the Krishna Rao Committee recommendations of 1975. However, any assessment made on the basis of organisational restructuring is incomplete, as it merely provides the skeletal framework for undertaking major military change. Organisations derive their ability to undertake concerted action on the basis of strategic direction, which guides the employment of an army in war. Therefore, in the given context, this chapter argues that military change has only been successful when it has been accompanied by successful strategic shifts, which harness the potential of organisational changes and provide them with the requisite direction, means and objectives for implementation. This includes the ability to outline realistic and considered goals by the political leadership.

The chapter analyses three case studies to highlight the importance of strategic changes. Two of these co-relate with the organisational shifts discussed in the previous chapter. The third analyses the 2004 Indian Army doctrine, with specific reference to Cold Start, the term often employed colloquially to describe the shift and discusses strategic change in relative isolation, even though it was not accompanied by major organisational shifts in the structure of the army. This helps assess the argument in reverse i.e. the possibility of successful military change with changes in strategy, even with limited structural changes.

Changes after the 1962 Sino-Indian War

The defeat at the hands of the Chinese in 1962 necessitated a change in strategy to deal with the threat that continued to remain relevant even after their unilateral withdrawal in November 1962. Jawaharlal Nehru foresaw the threat from China as a long-term concern.[1] He therefore envisaged the build-up of defence capability and world opinion in India's favour over a period of time. He wanted an increase in defence capability through not only the enhancement of the army's capacity, but also the defence industrial base, which could support it. Given the criticality of the situation, Nehru also pushed for immediate steps to procure defence equipment for the army from countries like the US, erstwhile USSR and UK.[2]

After 1962, India was able to clearly establish a strategic linkage between defence against China, especially in the Ladakh sector, and the criticality of retaining Kashmir as a firm base.[3] It was realised that if India lost control of the Kashmir Valley, it would not be able to defend Ladakh in case of renewed hostilities. Therefore, defence of India, and specifically Jammu and Kashmir (J&K) became closely linked with not only Pakistan but also China.

At the peak of the crisis, the possibility of an air defence pact was also explored with the US. This was based on the premise that India would prepare airfields and man the radars, while the US would provide aircraft for the defence of population centres.[4] This would have been a major departure from the existing policy, which did not even allow the employment of Indian air assets against China. Given the sensitivity of such a proposal, Nehru cloaked it as provision of air support in case of an emergency by friendly countries. This did not entail the permanent stationing of US air assets, thereby achieving the intended aim.[5] However, this policy did not come into force and the change was limited to the decision to employ Indian air assets in case of fresh hostilities by the Chinese.[6]

Gradually, over the course of time, Pakistan and China strengthened their relationship. This led to a clear enunciation of the duality of threat emerging from the west and north of India. It entailed earmarking of not only dedicated forces in a defensive posture in the vicinity of the border, but also demanded separate reserves and in case of Pakistan, offensive forces to be earmarked.

The army, while implementing government policy, made adjustments to its deployment in pursuit of its defensive strategy. Its initial strategy after the War clearly aimed at a defensive deployment, which was understandable given its larger role. However, rather than the deployment merely being defensive, it was afflicted with paranoia. The army ensured that the Chinese were not provoked by its deployment, even as the army had clearance under the Colombo Agreement after the War, which allowed it to occupy positions in vicinity of the McMahon line. Despite the government clearly mandating the forward deployment of the army in the North-East Frontier Agency (NEFA; now Arunachal Pradesh), it was stalled and delayed by the army. The sequence of events suggests that this was primarily aimed at avoiding even the slightest semblance of a threatening posture against the Chinese.[7] This led to the army undertake a static positional defensive deployment in Assam, with large parts of NEFA devoid of forces, exposing the vulnerability of the country, in case of any future attack. Major General D.K. Palit gives documentary evidence of this military policy, and quotes from the Emergency Cabinet Secretariat of January 29, 1963:

> PM agrees that: there is no objection in principle to Army Units and Assam Rifles going into NEFA and various points ... should not move into the disputed areas of Long-ju and Thag-la ... As regards Towang ... preliminary investigations into the possibility of locating some troops in this area may be undertaken ... Army's programme ... should, when it is ready, be cleared with him before it is actually implemented.[8]

This was followed up by a communication by the Army Headquarters to Headquarters Eastern Command vide its letter number 62718/GS/MO-1 of February 9, 1963. In contrast, it read:

> According to the Colombo Conference proposals, which have been accepted by the Government, the Indian Army is free to move up to NEFA/Tibet border ... (but)
>
> In accordance with the policy given out by the COAS [Chief of the Army Staff], we will give battle to the enemy *in the plains* for the present, due to our various difficulties. However, there is a requirement to move up into the areas vacated by us *for training* ... In fact it is vital that Assam Rifles move into their posts soon ... provided it is logistically possible.

> Recent operations in the area have brought out clearly our inability to maintain adequately the troops deployed there. No regular army units will, therefore, be moved up until they can be maintained by land routes ....[9] (Emphasis by Palit)

This communication is supported by the contents of the Colombo Conference on December 10-12, 1962 and further clarifications given on January 13, 1963. It clearly stated the following:

> The Indian forces can, in accordance with the Colombo Conference proposals, move right unto the south of the line of control, i.e. the McMahon Line, except for the two areas on which there is difference of opinion between the Governments of India and China.[10]

These two areas referred to were the Thagla ridge and Longju area, as mentioned above.

Major changes in the organisational structure of the army after the 1962 War primarily led to an increase in size and raising of mountain divisions. There was also enhanced stress on mountain warfare. However, as is apparent from literature of this period, there was little change in the strategic orientation of the army, which continued to remain not only defensive, but also incapable of best employing the upgraded state of organisational restructuring, which included a substantial increase in the strength of the army. Instead of employing the specialised mountain divisions and the larger numbers now available, the deployment clearly hinted at the propensity to avoid the remotest possibility of a military face off.

This approach was further affected by the inability of the army to adapt to changing methods of warfare. Its approach was beset by the positional trench warfare of the Second World War, which in the absence of requisite numbers, opened it to easily being bypassed given the characteristics of the mountainous terrain. An assessment of these tactics led both Galbraith and General Kelly, Chief of U.S. Military Supply Mission to India, to conclude that the deployment was "rather static and easily capable of being bypassed".[11] Galbraith goes on to suggest:

> Some of the generals were hoping that the Chinese will change their ways and attack along the roads like civilised people. They will seek out the Indians rather than outflank and bypass them. However, General

> Singh was quick to say that the disposition made no sense and they had every intention of correcting it.
>
> All this confirms my view of the Indian Army. It is competent and professional, but in some parts tragically old-fashioned.[12]

The ensuing military strategy, which witnessed deployment of brigades in the plains of Assam reinforced this thinking. Over the years, despite an evolving situation, the fear of Chinese offensive into India and the Indian Army's defensive approach was further strengthened by the decision to keep border infrastructure, especially road development at a minimal scale. The decision was guided by the understanding that it would prevent the possibility of Chinese forces exploiting it, in case of yet another attack on Indian territory. This policy remained in force, leading to the loss of at least three decades, while China improved its communication network. This also led to the border population being robbed of the fruits of India's economic progress. From a strategic perspective, even when India did decide to raise additional forces for the sector, the constraints of infrastructure, especially road networks, all but made these force accretions redundant. Reiterating the same, former defence minister, A.K. Antony, stated on the floor of parliament: "I have no hesitation to say that China is in a better position than India in terms of border infrastructure. It is a mistake, it is all of us who are to be held collectively responsible for it. It is a historical legacy ...."[13]

This limitation was also driven by the inexperience of military leaders, who were primarily exposed to tactical operations during the Second World War and the conflict with Pakistan in 1947-48. The rapid, accelerated promotions of officers in the senior ranks after Partition, gave them limited understanding of these issues, which could have been important factors for implementing the requisite changes. Evidence of this limitation is further apparent from the writings of the period, which despite the setback faced had not evolved into the strategic domain. The United Service Institution of India (USI)'s December 1962-1966 issues of the *USI Journal of India*, a premier platform for military writing, clearly highlight the focus on tactical issues, with the exception of a few voices advocating a paradigm shift in warfare. Particularly, the need for enhancing air mobility and special forces, which could well have provided the much needed flexibility to the army, instead of the deep-rooted defensive strategy that was adopted.[14]

Though this very inexperience was in a way responsible for providing direction to the post-1962 military change, however, it was again in evidence during the 1965 Indo-Pak War, too. It was an illustration of limited strategic direction, which constrained achievement of an outright victory, instead of the stalemate that the war eventually ended in. Reinforcing this reality, Lt Gen. Harbakhsh Singh, in an objective assessment of the 1965 Indo-Pak War wrote that the failure of leadership to achieve major strategic gains was due to "a faulty strategic concept of the campaign which resulted in a number of ineffective jabs instead of a few selective thrusts in force. In consequence, there were fierce slugging matches spread over a vast area in which we destroyed each other's potential but reached no strategic decisions".[15] He goes on to admit that even during the 1965 War, given the limitations of an unfavourable equipment profile vis-à-vis Pakistan, as also before that against China, even though some offensive plans did exist, the "bias was on the defensive. This induced in the majority of our commanders an unconscious attitude of defence-mindedness".[16] Thus, such a mindset makes apparent the self-imposed constraints of the army.

The army also failed to enhance its war-fighting capacity through newer ways and means. This led to the organisational changes that improved capabilities against perceived adversaries marginally, in the absence of an accompanying strategic shift. As quoted earlier, the means required to obviate existing challenges of terrain, like ingenious employment of air assets and special forces, witnessed limited incorporation. This led to stunted evolution in the structure and strategic thought of the army during this period.

Not only was the maturity of strategic thought in the army underdeveloped, the ability to evolve joint strategic concepts was severely constrained. This led the army, navy and air force to fight their independent battles, with little in terms of joint planning and integration of doctrinal thought. Interestingly, contrary to common perception, which suggests that thinking on the subject had not evolved adequately, the importance of the same was not only being reinforced at the highest level in the armed forces, but was also the subject of analysis within the intellectual domain. Air Chief Marshal P.C. Lal writes, "The bare facts of the matter are that in 1962 the Army and the Air Force did not fight together, and whatever operational plans were made were those of the Army alone. It was as if the Army was still thinking and fighting as it did in 1948. Habits die hard."[17] Commander K. Sridharan, writing in 1967, raised the possibility of combining the armed forces. Amongst the advantages that he visualised were, unity of command, responsive decision-making, unity of purpose, common doctrine and reduction of costs.[18] Each of these factors is as relevant today as it was then. Unfortunately, the armed forces still have a long way to go in the achievement of any of these objectives.

The inadequacy of military strategy was accompanied and caused to a great extent by limitations of formulating a national security strategy as well. This has been emphasised repeatedly by highly regarded men in uniform, who had the opportunity to be closely associated with the security planning architecture of the country. General Sundarji, elaborated on this limitation during the 1992 National Security Lecture at United Service Institution of India, with specific reference to the Nehruvian disdain for military matters.[19] He quoted Manekshaw, who re-emphasised Indian weakness in formulating a long-term strategy. Further, he said,

> Strategy involves the management of all resources of the Country, not only for the security of the State but also for its advancement, and for the fulfilment of hopes and aspirations of its people. To this end it is essential to formulate policy with a long term concept in mind. This regretfully was not done in the Nehru era ... The Shastri era was too short ... With Indira Gandhi ... much was achieved ... but infighting ... and the distrust ... preventing the evolvement (sic) of any long term strategy.[20]

K. Subrahmanyan was also critical of the government's inability to outline its assessment of the international situation, absence of a national security doctrine and getting a feedback on security policies from external non-governmental institutions, which according to him led to the inability to develop a coherent approach to security.[21]

Changes Post 1975 Krishna Rao Recommendations

Military change based on the 1975 reforms cannot be seen in isolation as an exercise in modernisation of the armed forces. The process was preceded by shifts in military and geopolitical realities, which led to these changes.

The most profound military event, which impacted the strategic shift was India's victory in the 1971 Indo-Pak War. The dismemberment of Pakistan and the ensuing effect on its war-waging potential created conditions which favoured the maintenance of territorial status quo from India's perspective. This implied that India no longer aimed to take the war to its adversary, since breakup of the erstwhile West Pakistan was not in its interest. India was thus a "satisfied regional power" at this stage of history.[22] The resultant impact of the War also moved India from the status of a co-equal of Pakistan in terms of conventional military capability, to a superior power. Some would go as far as to suggest that prior to the 1971 War, Pakistan had developed a clear edge in military capabilities, as was evident during the 1965 Indo-Pak War.[23] The defeat in 1971, along with the humiliating surrender of over 90,000 personnel, virtually eliminated Pakistan's ability to employ conventional conflicts as a means of changing the status quo and wresting Kashmir from India, which was its foremost objective for 25 years since independence.

The War also highlighted the limits of military support that Pakistan could expect from major powers including the US and China. The instances of sabre rattling during the War were exposed, with little in terms of direct military involvement emerging in the process. This was accompanied by the 1971 Treaty of Peace, Friendship and Cooperation between India and erstwhile USSR, which created a diplomatic balance and offset the pressures from China and the US.

The favourable conditions created after the War, however, came under stress soon thereafter. The evolving geopolitical situation increased the strain on India's economy. The 1973 Arab-Israel War saw the West Asian countries constrict supply of oil, which in turn resulted in an increase in oil prices, adversely affecting India's economic burden.[24] This negatively impacted the ability of the state to fund military modernisation efforts. In addition to these financial limitations, the fast-paced growth of the Pakistani Armed Forces and supply of weapons by China led to increasing concerns within the Indian security establishment. This was reinforced by Bhutto's commitment to "build up Pakistan's Armed Forces as 'the finest fighting force in Asia'".[25] It resulted in Pakistan augmenting its armed forces to levels beyond those available in 1971. At this stage, Pakistan's allocation for the armed forces was 50 per cent of the national budget and 10 per cent of the Gross National Product.[26]

These developments led to the need for fiscal consolidation in general and achieving greater efficiency in defence expenditure in particular.[27] Improvement in military efficiency could best be achieved by improving the teeth to tail ratio of the armed forces. There was a simultaneous need to create a paradigm shift in its strategic thought, if the army were to obviate the virtual stalemate along its Western border during the previous two wars. This became one of the cornerstones of the 1975 Krishna Rao Committee report, as noted by Rao himself.[28]

Between fiscal consolidation and enhancing military capability, the latter was a more challenging task in light of Pakistan's modernisation efforts and limited budgets. Constraints were imposed by a virtual military stalemate and reliance on positional warfare, as a result of Pakistan's strategy to obviate its limited depth by erecting a series of obstacle systems in the plains of Punjab. This led to a reassessment of what had essentially become an attrition-oriented approach to warfare. This limited the depth of India's counteroffensive during the 1965 Indo-Pak War and the challenge became all the more formidable by 1971. The layout of defensive fortifications along linear obstacles, in the form of canals and *ditch-cum-bundh* obstacle systems, constrained the manoeuvre space for mechanised elements and imposed a number of limitations in terms of time and casualties to the progress of battle. These obstacle systems were located between the international border and value objectives, in terms of towns, irrigation headworks, major road networks and industrial centres.[29] This practically ensured a painstaking fight through build-up-areas in the vicinity of the border between opposing forces, which was bound to become prohibitive in terms of manpower and equipment casualties.

These limitations had become a subject of assessment even before the 1971 War, given the challenges faced during the 1965 War and the ensuing military developments in Pakistan thereafter. Writing in 1967, Brig Sheodan Singh reinforced the importance of armour as a strategic weapon of choice, which if employed with due deliberation, could provide decisive results: "... The main aim should be to deliver the enemy hard blows in his vital but soft areas, the loss of which will throw him off balance and incapacitate him for further operations, or at least seriously jeopardise the progress of his subsequent operations if the move is timely and unexpected."[30] However, the army was still to fully exploit the open desert sector until this stage, as was witnessed during the 1965 War. Yet, the evolution of concepts had begun, emphasising the need for opening the battlefield to allow more elbow room to manoeuvre elements in the army.

Soon after the 1971 War, the thought process towards creating a shift in India's strategic posture became even more pronounced, given the experience in the western theatre, which had witnessed the constraints of fighting in the developed areas of the two countries. K Subrahmanyam wrote in 1972:

> If Pakistan is convinced that, in the case of war the Indian armoured force will not be used restrictively in Punjab only or will not be slowed down and stopped by well-prepared defence and water obstacles, then it will be deterred from invoking external support for its confrontation all the time and settle down to a policy of bilateralism. Consequently, India must develop armoured forces which can move across desert area, and also adequate and self-contained armoured forces which can strike across each doab and water crossing obstacles. Such forces must have medium tanks with water-crossing capability, self-propelled guns, fast-moving mechanised infantry with adequate anti-aircraft protection and bridging and mine-clearing capabilities.[31]

There were many influences on the ensuing approach adopted by the army. Foremost amongst these was the 1973 Yom Kippur War, which witnessed the impact of manoeuvre warfare and exploitation of battle space to turn the tide of the War in favour of Israel. A number of articles in professional journals appeared during this period, which proposed adoption of the same strategic principles applied during the War. An analysis of different aspects of the War, over a five year period, clearly indicates the impact of the same on the Indian Army and its evolving strategic thought, especially in terms of mechanised warfare. Foremost amongst the concepts that came up for debate was the ability of an army to undertake crossing a formidable obstacle, use of anti-tank weapons against a predominantly armour assault and employment of mechanised forces.[32] This was reiterated formally by the Government of India by endorsing it in the Ministry of Defence (MoD)'s *Annual Report: 1973-74*. It observed, "We have, in this connection, to take note of the lessons emerging from the West Asia war of October 1973, which provided the proving ground for some of the newest weaponry."[33] This thought process was further pollinated by the emulation of concepts that were being validated in the US Armed Forces during this period. The raising of the Reorganised Objective Army Division

(ROAD) was seen as a strong influence on Sundarji's decision to raise the Reorganised Army Plains Infantry Division (RAPID).[34]

It is not surprising that this churning within the army ran concurrent with the organisational changes that began formally in 1975. Together these related to India's national goals, emerging threats, advancement of technology and drove the army's strategic outlook, even as financial constraints were kept in mind while modernising.

In more specific terms, the 1975 expert committee faced the challenge of recommending modernisation within the existing strength of the Indian Army, which was limited to 8.378 lakh according to the MoD's *Annual Report: 1973-74*.[35] This constrained the ability of planners in light of the two-front threat from Pakistan and China, which they needed to address as part of their perspective planning. This was further related to the numerical balance, which was tilted against India (see Table 3) at this stage.

Table 3: Comparative Military Strength

(a)	West	Pakistan	India
	Armoured Divisions	2	2
	Mechanised Divisions	0	1
	Infantry Divisions	19	19
	Independent Armoured Brigades	8	5
	Independent Infantry Brigades	4	9
(b)	East	China	India
	Divisions	20-30	11

Note: In addition, Bangladesh had six Divisions.
Source: Gen. K.V. Krishna Rao, *Prepare or Perish: A Study of National Security*[36]

These numbers clearly indicate that India was in no position to create a substantial numerical advantage, in order to maintain a conventional military edge. The only option available was to build technological superiority and improve the army' capability. This dilemma is best captured by Krishna Rao:

> As has been brought out earlier, if offensive action is to be taken, after containing the enemy thrusts, generally a three to one superiority would be required for the counter offensive. In the case of Pakistan, this would mean increasing the strength of the Indian Army in the West to a considerable extent. Owing to financial constraints, this may not be possible. It would not be prudent to move forces from East to West

> either, as the forces deployed against China are the minimum required and it may be risky to denude the border. In any case, the force really comprises Mountain Divisions, which are not effective enough in the plains of the West, where the main fighting will take place. The option, therefore left, to tackle the problem in the West is to improve the quality of the forces in all respects, as opposed to quantity.[37]

However, according to Rao, the strategy continued to be oriented towards defence, with a strong capability to launch a counteroffensive after the attrition of the initial enemy offensive.[38] The strategy therefore could at best be described as *offensive defence*, which was a change from the defensive strategy that had been the basis of the army's planning until the 1971 War. Lt Gen. Sinha clearly visualised all past wars with Pakistan, as an illustration of India's defensive strategy, which included the 1971 Indo-Pak War, given the initial plan to establish a lodgement to settle Bangladeshi refugees.[39] This underwent a more offensive orientation for a short period, when Gen. Sunderji envisaged an offensive strategy based on the doctrine of compellence.[40] The same was attempted by India during Exercise Brasstacks and Operation Parakram, in an attempt to force Pakistan to stop the use of its territory for terrorism against India.[41]

The essential elements of the new strategy aimed at compelling Pakistan against continuing with its policy of destabilising India by putting a stop to its sponsorship of terrorism in Punjab during the eighties. The strategy could have also potentially been employed to undertake punitive strikes against future military threats, if the need arose. This could be achieved by developing a capability to cause severe destruction of the Pakistani war-waging potential in terms of its military capacity or even drive a wedge between Pakistani Punjab and Sind, which was an assessment based on Pakistani apprehensions and reading of the situation.[42] The means employed for this were spearheaded by a strong mechanised component of the army, superiority in fire power delivery, ability to support the operations logistically, through seamless communication systems, bridging capability, which could limit the deterrence potential of obstacles and the ability to fight equally well during day and night. More specifically, this included validation of RAPIDs, Army Radio Engineered Network (AREN) communications and the Tac C3I system, which was still in its infancy.[43]

The impact of the 1975 initiative in terms of a substantive military change, in the absence of its test in war, can best be judged by the adversary's objective assessment. The mid-eighties witnessed a number of exercises, some of which attempted to validate the strategic concepts initiated on the basis of military reforms. Amongst these, Exercise Brasstacks is possibly the best known, partly because it raised the possibility of an impending war between India and Pakistan.

Interviews conducted by Chari, Cheema and Cohen with Pakistani senior officers indicated their appreciation of the Indian Army's progression to mechanised predominant warfare, as well as its spinoffs. This included the belief that it was "something they would have done themselves". They felt that "the shift from a simple plains infantry division to a mechanised formation was believed to be a sensible move in purely military terms, even if it did create new problems for Pakistani planners".[44]

Therefore, purely from the strategic perspective, military change undertaken by the Indian Army had been successful in not only implementing major structural changes, but also creating an accompanying strategic framework, which could well have achieved its desired objectives if implemented. However, the window of implementation of these changes turned out to be narrow, as Pakistan not only let out the nuclear genie from their strategic options bag, but also put in place delivery mechanisms, which were still considered doubtful during Brasstacks.[45] The nuclear overhang cast its shadow over the subcontinent, especially with reference to a conventional military option against Pakistan. It was time for the next military change to create a strategic opening for India.

Cold Start or Limited Pre-emptive Offensive

The changing strategic scenario posed overwhelming limitations on an offensive into Pakistan, as part of the policy of deterrence by punishment or compellence, spearheaded by a large strike corps, as visualised in the seventies and eighties. The existing structure of the army, as well as its strategy validated during Brasstacks, was constrained on four counts.

First, the size of the strike element, distance from the intended area of operations and its accompanying limitations of speed led to lethargic mobilisation that all but took away any advantage that conventional superiority of force could afford. This argument was reinforced during Operation Parakram, when the armed forces were deployed on the borders in response to the terrorist strike on the Indian Parliament, clearly sponsored by Pakistani intelligence agency – the Inter-Services Intelligence (ISI).[46] The slow-paced mobilisation of the strike corps limited the potential dividends that an ideal offensive could have accrued to the country.

Second, the strike element presented a viable target in case Pakistan decided to employ nuclear weapons against India, in pursuit of its first-use policy. Thus, deployment became a challenge, virtually blunting the offensive capability. It also reinforced the army's inability to create options against sub-conventional threats of the kind employed by Pakistan in Punjab and J&K. The constraints worked in Pakistan's favour, based on the calculation that simmering temperatures generated by it as a result of the low intensity proxy war, would remain well below the threshold of two nuclear powers going to war over sponsorship of terrorism.

Third, the rigid structure of the formations, compartmentalised them into a strike and defensive role. This was not the best way of utilising limited resources required to be employed across a large border with Pakistan, with the added concern of a simultaneous threat from China.

Fourth, the conventional option had to be exercised in a manner that did not allow the justification of a nuclear exchange against strategic targets in India and yet be applied in pursuit of national objectives.

The conventional edge that had been created by the reforms of the eighties soon became a victim of the lost decade of military modernisation, given the severe economic constraints that were faced by the country in the nineties. This came to the fore during the Kargil conflict, leading the then Chief, General Malik, to say: "We shall fight with whatever we have."[47]

Despite limitations imposed by the poor state of weapons and equipment in the army, the Kargil conflict of 1999 was instructive in many respects. It witnessed a limited conflict with Pakistan under a nuclear overhang. Despite grave provocations of violation of the previous agreements by Pakistan and its overwhelmingly advantageous tactical positions occupied inside Indian territory, India chose to not only desist from enlarging the theatre of operations, it also placed a self-imposed term of reference to not cross the Line of Control (LoC). For the votaries of manoeuvre being synonymous with the vast open expanse of the desert, some of the operations conducted by the army became classical examples of tactical manoeuvre, which in their cumulative impact became a critical battle winning factor. The conflict also clearly illustrated the inability to accept loss of territory. According to General Malik, the army chief during the conflict, this made the very concept of trading territory a challenge. It thereby limited the ability to take losses at some place, in order to gain a much larger area elsewhere.[48]

Thus, a new strategy was needed in order to address all the limitations that had come to affect India's ability to generate strategic options within the conventional military sphere of war fighting. The solution required the army to retain a limited war option, negate the disadvantage of time differential in mobilisation, avoid the potential employment of nuclear weapons as a result of severely decapitating threat to Pakistani core interests, continue to pursue superiority in capability despite relative force parity and finally create smaller, flexible and faster offensive options instead of the strike corps.

The army attempted to develop these very capabilities through its doctrine released in early 2004. This doctrine was released in two versions. The unclassified document was available in public domain, while the classified one remained strictly for use within the armed forces.[49] The doctrine went on to highlight the need to "visualise and comprehend battles more clearly" a euphemism for strategic foresight, as the ideational desirable and tactical and operational superiority through information based manoeuvre warfare conducted in an all arms environment.

The doctrine visualised the need for the erstwhile "holding" or defensive corps to develop capabilities to undertake a dual role, wherein "minimum essential forces should be committed to holding vital areas and the remainder should be grouped, positioned and tasked to conduct offensive operations to improve the defensive posture and create 'windows of opportunity' for development of further operations".[50] This shift was accompanied by a simultaneous move to employ smaller battle groups from the strike corps with the aim of "being inserted into operational level battle, either as battle groups or as a whole, to capture or threaten strategic and operational objective(s) with a view to cause destruction of the enemy's reserves and capture sizeable portions of territory".[51]

The doctrine also re-emphasised the need to reduce the period of mobilisation. This was a clear reference to the limitations observed during

Operation Parakram: "All planning should aim to mobilise forces in the minimum possible time in order to take advantage of the many benefits that such a step offers."[52] It further highlighted the option of a limited war as part of the conventional domain of war fighting, which became clearer over a period of time, including the conditions under which such operations might be undertaken. In this context, General Deepak Kapoor listed the possible triggers for a limited war as: an intrusion into Indian territory like Kargil; border skirmishes escalating into larger conflicts; and finally, "limited war may also need to be initiated by India as a proactive limited response to continuing proxy war or a high profile terrorist incident, which requires immediate response".[53] He also felt that this option presented the advantage of undertaking a military option, without crossing the nuclear threshold. Kapoor went on to flag the need for identifying and neutralising the centre of gravity and having "clearly defined and understood aims for the intended operations". Finally, he felt that "proactive surgical operations, designed to achieve objectives quickly and decisively at least cost, will be the key to win limited wars".[54] Without elaborating on the options available, in 2008, then foreign minister, Pranab Mukherjee, also underscored the option of "protecting its territorial integrity and take appropriate action as and when it feels necessary" in the wake of ISI sponsored terrorist strikes in Mumbai.[55]

In addition to the doctrinal changes, the army attempted strategic shifts, with an aim of obviating the nuclear dilemma. While it was never formally articulated by the Indian Army, informed analysts indicated the employment of a strategy which involved an offensive across multiple fronts, by battle groups, with the aim of capturing shallow objectives.[56] This generated an option below the existing nuclear threshold, thereby upsetting Pakistan's erstwhile strategic nuclear weapons capability.

This strategy led to immense churning within the Pakistani military and strategic community.[57] Pakistan conducted a series of exercises named *Azm-e-Nau* or "New Resolve" from 2010 to 2013, both as wargames and physical manoeuvres involving troops. It was clear from information emanating from Pakistan "that capabilities of Pak Army will act as force multipliers by reducing the fog of war for own troops, obviating enemy surprise and reducing own reaction time".[58] This was reinforced by Lieutenant General Khalid Kidwai, the former head of the National Command Authority for 15 years. He felt that "Pakistan took the doctrine seriously" as it had a direct bearing on its security.[59] This was obviously in relation to India's doctrine, with an aim of neutralising the perceived advantage that it seemed to have afforded to the Indian Army.

Besides the conventional changes undertaken by Pakistan, shifts were also made in the nuclear domain. Kidwai pointed out that Pakistan went in for tactical nuclear weapons and the requisite delivery mechanism to offset the sudden opening developed by India in the tactical sphere. He said:

> And when you are trying to hit Pakistan within 48 to 96 hours with tactical formations, eight to nine of them simultaneously, you are obviously looking at gaps on our side on the tactical nuclear weapons. Therefore, the idea of Nasr was born, that we need to plug this particular gap, which is encouraging, or driving this particular doctrine. And so Nasr was created, and by the grace of God it has been a great success, as all leaders have confirmed. And we hope, therefore, that the complete spectrum that we say, the full spectrum, strategic, operational, tactical, all three levels of nuclear weapons have been covered, and therefore we have now deterred – in our thinking – the tactical level operations under the Cold Start Doctrine as well.[60]

Pakistan, as a result, shifted from a declared credible minimum deterrence posture to that of "full spectrum deterrence".

In 2010, then Army Chief, General V.K. Singh said that India did not have a "Cold Start" doctrine.[61] While the details of India's strategic options understandably remain classified, yet, it is clear that despite the flutter created by Cold Start, the options of undertaking a conventional strike by either of the nuclear armed countries have since receded. India's decision to not employ this option after 26/11 has further reinforced this reality.

The changes as a result of the 2004 doctrine took place after the experience of Operation Vijay in Kargil and Operation Parakram. While the army did undertake some organisational restructuring on the basis of its experiences, these, as highlighted in the Chapter 2, were aimed more at improving command and control and employment of available resources. The military change undertaken, therefore, was primarily strategic in nature. It is also evident from Pakistan's reaction that the changes were reasonably successful in forcing a rethink of existing force structures, location of military formations and nuclear deterrence options.

NOTES

1. Jawaharlal Nehru, "February 2, 1963", in G. Parthasarthi (ed.), *Letters to Chief Ministers: 1947-1964, Vol 5 1958-1964*, Oxford University Press, Delhi, 1989, p. 566.
2. See R.D. Pradhan, *Debacle to Resurgence: Y. B. Chavan Defence Minister (1962-1966)*, Atlantic Publishers, New Delhi, 2013. The author devotes a chapter each to Chavan's visits to the three countries in a bid to buy weapons for the three services.
3. Sarvepalli Gopal, *Jawaharlal Nehru: A Biography*, Oxford University Press, New Delhi, 2010, p. 448.
4. John Kenneth Galbraith, *Ambassador's Journal*, Hamish Hamilton, London, 1969, p. 504.
5. Ibid., p. 551. Based on a clarification given by Nehru in the Parliament on the issue of an "air umbrella".
6. Maj. Gen. D.K. Palit, *War in the High Himalayas*, Lancer International, New Delhi, 1991, p. 415.
7. Ibid., pp. 416 and 419.
8. Ibid., p. 386.
9. Ibid., pp. 386-387.
10. Gen. K. V. Krishna Rao, *Prepare or Perish: A Study of National Security*, Lancer Publishers, New Delhi, 1991, pp. 478-479.
11. John Kenneth Galbraith, No. 4, p. 506.
12. Ibid., pp. 506-507. General Singh refers to Lt Gen. Harbakhsh Singh who took over as the 04 Corps Commander.
13. "China Fears India's Infra Build-up at LAC: AK Antony", *DNA*, September 7, 2013, at http://www.dnaindia.com/india/report-china-fears-indias-infra-build-up-at-lac-ak-antony-1885602 (Accessed July 9, 2015).
14. Maj. Gen. S.K. Sinha, "Army-Air Corps", *USI Journal of India*, LXXXXIV (395), April-June 1964, pp. 136-138; Maj. V. R. Raghavan, "Special Forces for Northern Frontiers", *USI Journal of India,* LXXXXIV (395), April-June 1964, pp. 122-126.
15. Lt Gen. Harbakhsh Singh, *War Despatches: Indo-Pak Conflict 1965*, Lancer International, New Delhi, 1991, p. 193.
16. Ibid., pp. 7-8.
17. Air Chief Marshal P.C. Lal, *Some Problems of Defence*, United Service Institution of India, New Delhi, 1977, p. 69.
18. Commander K. Sridharan, "Should India Unify Its Armed Forces?", *USI Journal of India*, LXXXXVII (408), July-September 1967, pp. 248-249.
19. General K. Sundarji, "USI National Security Lecture 1992: The World Power Structure in Transition from a Quasi Unipolar to a Quasi Multipolar State and the Options of a Middle Power in the Milieu", United Service Institution of India, New Delhi, 1993, p. 24.
20. Ibid., pp. 24-25.
21. See K. Subrahmanyam, "Does India Have a Strategic Perspective?", in K. Subrahmanyam and Arthur Monteiro, *Shedding Shibboleths: India's Evolving Strategic Outlook*, Wordsmiths, New Delhi, 2005, pp. 7-15.
22. Ali Ahmed, *India's Doctrine Puzzle: Limiting War in South Asia*, Routledge, New Delhi, 2014, p. 39.
23. Gen. K.V. Krishna Rao, No. 10, p. 405.
24. *Annual Report: 1973-1974*, Ministry of Defence, New Delhi, pp. 1-2. According to Michael L. Ross, in an article in *Foreign Affairs*, the initial shock was felt as a result of a 70 per cent increase in oil prices in 1973 and by March 1974, the price of a barrel of oil had gone up

four times to $ 12. See Michael L. Ross, "How the 1973 Oil Embargo Saved the Planet: OPEC Gave the Rest of the World a Head Start against Climate Change", *Foreign Affairs,* October 15, 2013, at https://www.foreignaffairs.com/articles/north-america/2013-10-15/how-1973-oil-embargo-saved-planet (Accessed July 16, 2016). For the direct impact on India, see: Mihir Rakshit, "Some Macroeconomics of Oil Price Shocks", *ICRA Bulletin,* December 2011, at http://www.icra.in/Files/MoneyFinance/mihirrakshit.pdf (Accessed July 16, 2015).

25. Ibid. (*Annual Report: 1973-1974*), p. 3.
26. Ibid.
27. Ibid., pp. 14-21. The *1973-74 Annual Report* of the Ministry of Defence conveys at length the steps initiated to improve defence management. These included improvement in procedures for threat analysis and judging requirements based on it, and the advent of computerisation for enhancing efficiency, better inventory management, project management and use of consultants from outside the services.
28. Gen. K.V. Krishna Rao, No. 10, p. 406.
29. For better understanding of Pakistan's obstacle systems, especially the canals and their obstacle value, see: Rohit Vats, "Pakistan Defence-Canals in South Punjab and Sindh - 1 (Sulemanki-Fort Abbas)", *Perspective,* at http://vatsrohit.blogspot.in/2012/08/pakistan-defensive-canals-in-south.html (Accessed July 17, 2015).
30. Brig. Sheodan Singh, "Employment of Armour - Some Aspects", *USI Journal of India,* LXXXXVIII (406), January-March 1967, p. 60.
31. K. Subrahmanyam, *Our National Security,* Economic and Scientific Research Foundation, New Delhi, December 1972, p. xxv.
32. Maj. Gen. S.K. Sinha, "Suez Crossings", *USI Journal of India,* CIV (436), July-September 1974, pp. 219-226; Edgar O'balance, "Yom Kippur War", *USI Journal of India,* CIV (434), January-March 1974, pp. 7-16; Maj. D. K. Kanwar, "The Egyptian Counter Across the Suez – 1973", *USI Journal of India,* CVII (447), April-June 1977, pp. 108-116; Brig. B. S. Sirohi, "Arab-Israeli War of October 1973", *USI Journal of India,* CVIII (451), January-March 1978, pp. 20-45; S. S. Srivastava, "Use of Tank and Anti-Tank Weapons in the Arab Israeli War of 1973", *USI Journal of India,* CIX (457), July-September 1979, pp. 247-259.
33. *Annual Report: 1973-1974,* No. 24, p. 12.
34. Ali Ahmed, No. 22, p 42.
35. *Annual Report: 1973-1974,* No. 24, p. 22.
36. Gen. K.V. Krishna Rao, No. 10, p 405.
37. Ibid.
38. Ibid.
39. Lt Gen. S.K. Sinha, "Threats and Strategy", in Maj. Gen. Rajendra Nath, Shyam Khosla and Ashok Malik (eds.), *Indian Security: Threats and Strategies,* Panchnad Research Institute, Chandigarh, 1990, p. 51.
40. See Ali Ahmed, No. 22, p. 44.
41. This initiative, while extracting a statement from Pakistan, failed to ensure compliance. See Gaurav Kampani, "India's Compellence Strategy: Calling Pakistan's Nuclear Bluff over Kashmir", Monterey Institute of International Studies, March 2002, at http://cns.miis.edu/stories/020610.htm (Accessed July 16, 2015).
42. Vergese Koithara, *Crafting Peace in Kashmir: Through a Realist Lens,* Sage Publications, New Delhi, 2004, p. 42; also see P. R. Chari, Pervaiz Iqbal Cheema and Stephen P. Cohen, *Four*

Crises and a Peace Process: American Engagement in South Asia, Brookings Institution Press, Washington, 2007, p. 48.

43. Ibid. (P. R. Chari, Pervaiz Iqbal Cheema and Stephen P. Cohen), pp. 44-45.
44. Ibid., p. 48.
45. W.P.S. Sidhu, *India's Security and Nuclear Risk Reduction Measures*, at http://www.stimson.org/images/uploads/research-pdfs/sidhufnl.pdf, p. 39 (Accessed March 16, 2016).
46. J.T. Vishnu, "ISI supervised Parliament Attack, Main Coordinator of Jaish, Two Others Arrested", *The Tribune*, December 16, 2001, at http://www.tribuneindia.com/2001/20011217/main1.htm (Accessed March 17, 2016).
47. The remark came as a reaction to the unfortunate reality of severe shortages in weapons, equipment and ammunition faced by the army. See Gen. V.P. Malik, *Kargil: From Surprise to Victory*, Harper Collins, New Delhi, 2006, p. 289.
48. Ibid., p. 354.
49. *Indian Army Doctrine*, Army Training Command, Shimla, October 22, 2004, at ids.nic.in/Indian%20Army%20Doctrine/indianarmydoctrine_1.doc (Accessed July 1, 2015).
50. Ibid., p. 9.
51. Ibid., pp. 9-10.
52. Ibid., p. 5.
53. Gen. Deepak Kapoor (retd), "Limited Wars in the Indian Context", *India Strategic*, February 2012, at http://www.indiastrategic.in/topstories1368_limited_wars_in_the.htm (Accessed July 16, 2015).
54. Ibid.
55. Rahul Bedi, "India Says It Reserves Right to Attack If Territory under Threat", *The Irish Times*, December 3, 2008, at http://www.irishtimes.com/news/india-says-it-reserves-right-to-attack-if-territory-under-threat-1.918221 (Accessed July 22, 2015).
56. See Brig. Arun Sahgal, "Cold Start: New Doctrinal Thinking in the Army", *CLAWS Journal*, Summer 2008, at http://www.claws.in/images/journals_doc/1370052420_ArunSeghal.pdf (Accessed March 23, 2016).
57. See Stephen P. Cohen and Sunil Dasgupta, *Arming without Aiming: India's Military Modernization*, Viking, New Delhi, 2010, p. 66.
58. Brig. Dr Muhammad Khan, "From Cold Start to Cold Storage", Inter Services Public Relations, at https://www.ispr.gov.pk/front/main.asp?o=t-article&id=87 (Accessed July 21, 2015).
59. Peter Lavoy, "A Conversation with Gen. Khalid Kidwai", Carnegie International Nuclear Policy Conference 2015, Carnegie Endowment for International Peace, March 23, 2015, at http://carnegieendowment.org/files/03-230315carnegieKIDWAI.pdf#sthash.FisvunVj.dpuf (Accessed July 15, 2015).
60. Ibid., p. 9.
61. "India Has No 'Cold Start' Doctrine: Army Chief", rediff.com, December 02, 2010, at http://www.rediff.com/news/report/india-has-no-cold-star-doctrine-says-army-chief/20101202.htm (Accessed July 22, 2015).

4

Assessment of Military Change in a Conventional Environment

The fundamental question that arises based on the case studies discussed in the previous chapters is: What were the drivers for military change and what leads to successful military change? Or conversely, what led to the failure of the Indian Army to change, if it was indeed the case? The assessment of these two critical factors will provide a better understanding of triggers for change and the conditions that facilitate its successful culmination. Since the factors are solely related to the case studies, these could well be limited in scope. However, they do provide a guideline for understanding military change in the Indian context better, especially in case of conventional threats and the changes resulting therefrom.

Drivers of Military Change

The drivers for military change after the 1962 War were quite clearly the military defeat at the hands of China and the emerging operational environment. These led not only the military but also the political leadership to undertake changes that were aimed at restructuring the army. The objective of these changes was to ensure that the army was capable of defending the country against any future Chinese aggression. The overall structure of the army was also dictated by a potential two-front war, envisaged as part of the threat assessment. This was based on "growing rapprochement" between China and Pakistan[1] and was further strengthened when both countries reached a boundary agreement in the Kashmir area, held by Pakistan in early 1963.[2] According to Nehru, both China and Pakistan saw India as a common impediment and their interests were bound to converge in this regard.

> For the present, both these countries (Pakistan and China) feel that the major impediment in their way is India; therefore both have the common objective of doing injury to India and humiliating her so that in future they can proceed for realising their aims without this major obstacle.[3]

This assessment was reinforced by former US Ambassador to India, John Kenneth Galbraith, who questioned Pakistani inclusion in the Southeast Asia Treaty Organisation (SEATO) and Central Treaty Organisation (CENTO), even as the Chinese were "forming some kind of an axis with Pakistan".[4]

Unlike the changes after 1962, which took place after a defeat, as argued by Posen, the 1975 report came up under very different circumstances. It followed the most complete military victory by India in the 1971 Indo-Pak War. It is, therefore, important to underline the context of events and circumstances that preceded and succeeded the War, even as the changes were being implemented.

A scan of the international and regional environment provides a strategic backdrop to the changes envisaged. By 1971, Pakistan had become a frontline state of the US, having facilitated its overtures to China. This provided Pakistan additional leverage with the US, as well as closer ties with China. Thereafter, in a major turn of events, the former Soviet Union intervened in Afghanistan in 1979 and the US decided to contest the same through its proxies. In 1981, the Reagan government negotiated a $ 3.2 billion economic and military aid package for Pakistan.[5] It is not surprising that India's defence expenditure rose substantially from 1982-83, in order to maintain military balance with Pakistan.

The shifting balance of power in favour of Pakistan in the region led to a closer Soviet-India relationship. While this was initially evident during the signing of the 1971 Indo-Soviet Treaty of Peace, Friendship and Cooperation, subsequently, the relationship was strengthened by supply of arms to India by the erstwhile USSR on favourable terms. However, this relationship was aimed at defending India's security interests, rather than any military foray into Pakistan.[6]

India conducted a peaceful nuclear test in 1974. This became linked with Pakistan's growing determination to not only gain nuclear capability, but also pursue a nuclear weapons programme. Feroze Hassan Khan writes, "After India's nuclear test, Bhutto set the nuclear weapons program into high gear, and from 1974 onward it was the highest national security priority."[7]

According to Krishna Rao, the basis of the 1975 reforms process was inflationary pressures and rise in prices after the 1973 Arab-Israel War and the technological advancements witnessed during the War.[8] He also suggests that this process began with an aim of modernisation and more efficient utilisation of resources, as seen from the subsequent improvement in the teeth-to-tail ratio.[9] However, subsequent amendments to the perspective plan catered for "significant build-up and modernisation of the adversaries".[10]

Given the changing operational environment, the organisational changes undertaken were driven by the desire to transform the army's posture against Pakistan, from defensive to offensive-defence.[11] The 1971 War provided an ideal backdrop for building the army's military edge. While it was buoyed by a resounding victory, however, it was also clear from the series of battles in the western theatre of war that the ability to make substantial gains was increasingly becoming limited, as a result of extensive obstacle systems laid by Pakistan in the developed terrain, represented by the plains sector of Jammu and Punjab. It was perceived that the inability to make substantial gains in the Punjab sector could be offset by the option of pursuing mechanisation, which could militarily exploit the desert sector further south. The offensive potential of armour was augmented by the availability of world class technology from the former Soviet Union in the form of the BMP (Boyevaya Mashina Pekhoty) series – BMP-1, followed immediately thereafter by the BMP-2, the first Infantry Combat Vehicles (ICVs) in the world.[12]

Thus, the principal driver for military change after the 1962 War and 1975 reforms was not only the threat, but in a larger context, the overall *operational environment*. It is also clear from the changes post-1975 that the process was guided by the Krishna Rao committee report; however, it underwent gradual changes in accordance with the evolving security environment in India's neighbourhood. The changes post-1975, which eventually gained pace in the eighties, were supported by technological advances, especially related to the ICV platform. More importantly, India's defence relationship with the erstwhile Soviet Union, gave it a quantum jump in mechanised warfare.

The changes as a result of Pakistan's nuclearisation and its strategy of waging a proxy war against India led to the need to evolve options for a limited offensive, below the nuclear threshold. The operational environment led India to attempt a strategic bypass of its organisational and mobilisation time differential related limitations, by opting for the so-called Cold Start in 2004.

The operational environment of the period also led to a complementary shift in the doctrinal approach of the army. While there is inadequate evidence of such changes on the basis of official literature, yet the case studies suggest that the defensive doctrine after the 1962 War was gradually replaced by defensive deterrence, deterrence by punishment and finally bordering on compellence.[13] These changes became the overarching basis for related organisational restructuring during the period. In India's case, the operational environment emerges as the most important driver of military change. This is evident from the case studies analysed in Chapter 2 and 3.

Technology as a driver became more an enabler which facilitated the process of change. The most obvious example relates to the changes after the 1975 reforms, which led to the mechanisation of the army. In this case also, the changes were not revolutionary. These were undertaken more as emulation of Western influences and doctrines. The role of technology in changes after the 1962 War was comparatively limited.

Strategic culture underlines the response of a country to certain kinds of circumstances. The changes after 1962 can be characterised by a strategic culture which was essentially defensive. The organisational changes, too, reflected this phase of India's strategic evolution and were possibly shaped by its influence.[14] In India's case, this shift was evident during the 1971 Indo-Pak War, when a proactive India clearly displayed an offensive intent, which was substantially at variance from a passive and defensive strategic culture that had guided the country's actions. This can be considered a watershed in the evolutionary process of India's strategic culture. From a defensive orientation towards both Pakistan and China, India graduated to an offensive-defence approach against Pakistan. With time, the new-found confidence was also visible against China, though it took much longer for the Indian mindset of the sixties to undergo a change. Flashes of a proactive stance were evident in the eighties during Sundarji's leadership of the army, for example, in the military response to Pakistan, China and during the peacekeeping mission in Sri Lanka. However, over the years, this proactive policy could not sustain its tempo. Nonetheless, it is often suggested that the broader shift remained the basis for India's approach to its military adversaries, and became a clearly enunciated policy on the basis of the 2004 doctrine of the Indian Army. Reinforcing this argument, Ali Ahmed adds that the nuclear and conventional doctrines indicated a shift to an offensive strategic culture.[15] If this was indeed the case, then it could be identified as the third shift by India since independence.

However, this contention can be challenged on two counts. *First*, India has not been able to sustain the 2004 doctrine in the face of challenge by Pakistan, as seen during the 26/11 terrorist attack in Mumbai. *Second*, Cold Start, which was the basis for this doctrine for the army, has since been disowned and its efficacy remains uncertain.

Furthermore, the shifts suggest that strategic culture develops and matures with the passage of time. It is also cemented when threats and the reactions thereupon are dealt with a degree of predictability and an identifiable framework. In India, such a state is yet to be established with reasonable assurance. In its absence, it can be argued that India's strategic culture remains embedded in the policy of offensive defence which is implemented through the doctrine of deterrence by punishment at least in the case of Pakistan. Moreover, past attempts at military change are likely to be adversely affected in the absence of a complementary strategic culture, as changes are likely to remain attempts at paradigm shifts without the requisite conditions which support its implementation. The Cold Start doctrine is a case in point.

The army piggybacked on three factors, which supported the strategic shift and took it to a higher level.[16] *First*, India's economic liberalisation in the early 1990s led to a much faster rate of growth, which not only increased the scope for modernising the army, but also enhanced the status of India to an emerging economic powerhouse. Ironically, the economic factor is often seen as the reason for the inability of any military to grow. *Second*, India's decision to go nuclear in 1998 clearly declared its intent to bite the bullet in order to protect its strategic interests. This initially led to widespread outcry from major world powers. However, as the dust settled over its initial impact, India was able to successfully break out of its isolation, to emerge with substantially more strategic influence. *Third*, the Indo-US nuclear deal in 2005 took India's relations with the pre-eminent power in the world to a level wherein India's growing strategic status was further cemented. It also opened the possibilities of greater support for India's needs for advanced weapon systems and even joint development.[17]

India's doctrinal stance has been difficult to identify and define in the absence of its clear enunciation over the years. It is therefore equally challenging to illustrate its influence as a driver of military change. The changes post-1962 did not indicate a major doctrinal shift in case of the army. The 1971 Indo-Pak War brought about a shift in India's doctrine to deterrence by punishment, which continued after 1975. It was to that extent an illustration of a continuum after the War, wherein India maintained a posture of offensive defence against Pakistan. The limitations imposed, as a result of the factors discussed earlier, on India forced a rethink, which became the outcome of the 1975 report. The doctrine of deterrence by punishment could only have been implemented if the army created the requisite manoeuvre space for breaking out of the limitations imposed along the western front, especially in Punjab. This was achieved through the mechanisation of the army, along with the accompanying strategy of fast-paced operations with the capability of deep thrusts into enemy territory. The Sundarji doctrine, if one may describe it as such, further built on this foundation, indicating a shift towards compellence. However, the short period of its implementation limited its influence, which saw India slide back to deterrence. Subsequently, Operation Parakram also witnessed an attempt at achieving compellence, despite the ensuing limitations of implementing it. Therefore, while there was no change in India's doctrinal position after 1962, the 1975 changes pursued the doctrine of deterrence by punishment against Pakistan. Operation Parakram, and thereafter, Cold Start did attempt to implement compellence; however, its effect and success remain questionable.

Pathways of Military Change

Farrell and Terriff have suggested three pathways to military change. These include *emulation*, *adaptation* and *innovation*.[18] Innovation has been described as development of "new military technologies, tactics, strategies, and structures. Adaptation involves adjusting existing military means and methods". They go on to describe emulation as "incorporating new tools and ways of war through imitation of other military organisations".[19]

This framework can be tested through the cases analysed in this chapter. More importantly, it can provide inputs about the most common pathway employed for initiating change in the Indian context.

Amongst the two organisational changes, the introduction of mountain divisions, post-1962, was an adaptation of existing divisions employed in the plains. Tweaking of the existing structure and manpower resulted in lesser reliance on surface transport and the addition of animal transport instead. The utility of armour was limited in mountains, as was that of medium and heavy artillery. However, the adaptation could have well evolved further into innovation through incorporation of aviation assets and greater reliance on special forces, which despite all the years of its existence, failed to happen.

The organisational changes post-1975 were clearly an emulation of existing force structures in the US and European armies. However, since these were backed up by state-of-the-art equipment like BMP series, the resultant formation initially did border on innovation as well. However, this was constrained by the lack of resources in terms of aviation assets, matching mobility and logistics support structures.

The strategic changes were similar in their classification. *First*, the changes after 1962 witnessed limited adaptation from a strategic perspective, which resulted in the failure to best employ the additional resources and organisational structure created. *Second*, the strategic changes post-1975, much like the organisational shifts, were an example of emulation, drawing from Western concepts employed during the Cold War. *Third*, Cold Start was an adaptation of the existing strategy, wherein organisations were either restructured formally, as in the case of Pivot Corps, and informally, as seen with the Strike Corps, to create openings despite Pakistan's first-use nuclear policy.

This raises the question about the inability of the Indian Army to innovate, despite challenges including the threat from both China and Pakistan. Contrary to conventional understanding that this analysis seems to suggest, innovation has been difficult to achieve for other modern armies of the world as well. Armies and even organisations beyond the uniformed world, tend to rely more on emulation to replicate existing formulas of proven success. For example, North Atlantic Treaty Organisation (NATO)'s Combined Joint Task Force (CJTF), is based on the US concept of the JTF.[20] Similarly, organisational structures like the Chief of Defence Staff, Chairman Joint Chiefs of Staff Committee and theatre commanders have been emulated by a number of countries based on their successful implementation by the UK and the US.

If one relates this to the drivers for change, the Indian Army should have been pushing for change in the face of evolving threats from Pakistan and enlarging threat from China. However, it is the desire for status quo on part of India that limits its ability to innovate.[21] Even attempted changes like Cold Start and the creation of a corps against China have been constrained by inadequate consensus and resources, besides the limited potential of the changes, which are unlikely to fall within the purview of innovation.

Limitations with respect to technology are equally relevant. India has a weak defence technology base. This limits the ability of the army to base its innovations on a long-term timeline, which can be supported indigenously. In the absence of this capability, import of weapon systems is more often the norm rather than the exception. This implies that India remains well behind the curve in terms of induction of cutting-edge technology, especially given the procedural cycle of planning and procurement. It also ensures that the potential adversary, more often than not is either ahead of this curve, as is the case with China, or at least a co-equal, as is often seen in relation to Pakistan. Thus, the ability to innovate wrests more on strategic shifts, rather than technology-driven changes. This is also influenced more by adaptation and emulation, in the face of limited strategic breakthroughs emanating from the military intellectuals within the country. Possibly, for this reason concepts like manoeuvre warfare, fourth-generation warfare, hybrid warfare and procedures like systems approach to training and intelligence preparation of the battlefield have all been emulated and are an intrinsic part of the army's military lexicon.[22]

Desirables for Successful Change

Writing on the issue of formulating security policies, of which organisational restructuring is an integral part, K. Subrahmanyan relates weaknesses in our policymaking to five principle limitations. These include: a non-specialist political leadership; rapid turnover of services officers, thereby affecting their ability to conduct long-term planning; generalist civil service as well as intelligence services; and absence of a full-time focus by anyone in the government on national security.[23] With the establishment of the office of the National Security Advisor (NSA) and his affiliated secretariat, the last limitation has since been addressed; however, there is little change with regard to the others. In fact, tenures of senior officers in the army have only reduced further since Subrahmanyam wrote his piece.

The case studies, discussed previously, reinforce some of these aspects. However, this chapter enlarges the scope of desirables for successful change, and in certain cases, modifies it in order to relate it to existing realities. Amongst these, the desirability of a specialist bureaucracy and intelligence agencies is undeniable, as is the need for political leadership to have a more hands-on approach with regard to security issues. However, an attempt is made to look beyond these inherent limitations and focus on aspects which relate more to the specific domain of the armed forces.

For militaries to undertake successful military change, including restructuring of its organisational structure, the two case studies suggest the importance of the following:

- Long-term strategic assessment.
- Support from political establishment.
- Visionary and committed military leadership.
- Need for strong institutional structures.
- Follow-up action to take changes to their culmination.

In order to relate each of these requirements to the case studies and other associated conditions, a more detailed analysis of each is provided as follows:

Long-term Strategic Assessment

Major structural changes in an organisation must be based on net assessment, duly supported by high-grade intelligence, to analyse the challenges faced by the country. This in turn must become the foundation for its strategic assessment. Ideally strategic assessment must flow from national security imperatives as well as a periodic review of defence capabilities and threats. In the absence of a fountainhead of national security guidance, piecemeal and disconnected decision-making tends to replace a more structured approach to the vital imperative of strategic guidance. The immediate aftermath of the 1962 War witnessed a flurry of actions that aimed to make up critical shortfalls in equipment, weapons and manpower. However, there is little evidence that these were accompanied by a long-term strategic vision emanating from the top echelons of the government, despite an attempt by the then Defence Minister, Y.B. Chavan, to a limited extent, which could have guided the follow-up action of the armed forces. This echoed in the planning process of the army as well, which, further constrained by its weak institutional structures, could at best address its perceived immediate threats.

Weaknesses of intelligence agencies and institutions within the army, along with its operational follow-up, have posed serious limitations in the past. For example, the long list of demands given by the army to the US after the 1962 War to begin with, as suggested by both Palit and Taylor, were not rooted in the reality of the situation and resources available. The strategic assessment demanded by Chavan should have been the basis for the initial evaluation. Though ideally, this should have been preceded by a national security assessment of which the army and the armed forces were one of the important constituents.

The quality of some of these assessments remains questionable in light of structural weaknesses that continued to exist, despite efforts being made to overcome them after the 1962 debacle. The Joint Intelligence Committee (JIC), which reported to the Chiefs of Staff Committee, had already been found to be ineffective.[24] As a result, this was shifted to the Cabinet Secretariat. Moreover, despite the mandate to appoint an experienced intelligence officer as the head of JIC, according to Subrahmanyam, "the first available ICS officer due for promotion as Additional Secretary was made the JIC chairman".[25] A number of cases suggest that even where intelligence was available, the failure to carry out net assessment resulted in the inability to understand future challenges.

Limitations regarding intelligence-related operational assessment came to the fore in the immediate aftermath of the 1962 War only to be repeated again thereafter. A 2012 Institute for Defence Studies and Analyses (IDSA) Intelligence Task Force report suggests that problems exist with both civilian and military intelligence organisations. These include rigidity, lack of coordination and technical knowhow required in the context of modern-day warfare. It goes on to suggest:

> Most importantly, the external intelligence system is focussed more on political content, and less on military intelligence aspects. On the other hand, the military intelligence functions are confined to the services but have little authority to operate beyond tactical horizons.[26]

This anomaly clearly indicates the need for strengthening the military focus of external intelligence agencies and expanding the role of military intelligence agencies, both in terms of their role, resources available and upgrade of cadre capacity.[27]

Besides the specific challenge of intelligence gathering, and more importantly, its evaluation, it is equally important to integrate it as part of the army's long-term strategic net assessments. These assessments become the basis for perspective plans, which in turn will indicate the nature of organisational changes needed to maximise its benefits. This is best illustrated by the process of the army's mechanisation, which was accompanied by a thrust towards adopting tenets of modern warfare. The planning for the same commenced in 1975 and catered for the period till 2000.

The structured and systematic effort by the Krishna Rao committee led to a realistic assessment of future battlefield scenario. This was achieved by wide-ranging consultations by the committee and the professionalism of officers like Krishna Rao and Sundarji, who had the requisite understanding of matters strategic. The changes related to mechanisation correctly appreciated the limitations of attrition warfare by two armies which had near parity on the western front. Mechanisation facilitated manoeuvre and exploitation of the underdeveloped terrain of the deserts in order to overcome the heavy deployment and obstacle network of sensitive areas of Punjab. In contrast, General Chaudhari envisaged the "destruction of equipment" of the adversary, in the absence of other viable alternatives.[28]

These changes could take place as a result of the political leadership's clear understanding of the country's strategic direction, which is an essential pre-requisite for action by the army.[29] The army benefitted from this during the Sundarji era, which witnessed close cooperation between the political leadership and the army's top brass. However, even during this period, when this link broke, as was the case with the conduct of Operation Brasstacks, about which Rajiv Gandhi was possibly unaware, decision-making was compromised.[30]

The case study, while highlighting the importance of a clear strategic perspective, reinforces the need for a periodic review of the strategic assessment, as also a follow-up. These can best provide guidance to the armed forces if followed up as a regular feature and in the form of a tri-services vision, duly supported by both government and non-government institutions.

Support from Political Establishment

Very often, political leadership is considered the reason for existing weaknesses in India's defence structure, and therefore, also a reason for its inability to reform and change.[31] However, the two case studies suggest a different reality. Both instances of organisational restructuring were overseen by prudent and effective political leaders. Y.B. Chavan, despite his inexperience in matters related to defence, built a cohesive senior leadership and galvanised the armed forces.[32] He provided the necessary support for the expansion of the army and its equipping goals. Similarly, Rajiv Gandhi and Arun Singh were both closely involved with building the defence forces and supported the mechanisation process. Government representatives negotiated with countries, which supplied the necessary hardware for equipping newly raised formations of the army.[33] An attempt was made to build long-term capacity of the army through industrialisation of defence production, which was given the necessary impetus.[34]

Besides organisational changes, which could not have taken place without backing from the government, strategic shifts raise doubts in terms of governmental participation and guidance at the highest level. It was evident from Palit's account that differences existed in the policy of the government and its implementation by the army, in the strategic sphere after the 1962 War. While this dissonance was not tested in war, there is a likelihood that it could have led to reverses, under operational conditions. Similarly, there seem to have been serious differences regarding the strategic outlook of Sundarji and Rajiv Gandhi during Brasstacks, which has come to light on the basis of recent interviews. Reportedly, Rajiv Gandhi was not aware of the exact nature of the exercise and its potential implications.[35] This clearly indicates gaps in strategic decision-making, which becomes a limitation in undertaking military change. The controversy surrounding Cold Start is similar. It has been contended that the air force was not taken on board while formulating the doctrine, which subsequently led to differences over its implementation. Air Vice Marshal (Retd) Kapil Kak indicated the lack of consensus when he said, "There is no question of the air force fitting itself into a doctrine propounded by the army. This is a concept dead at inception."[36] Since the doctrine was released by the army, the level of political support for the same also remains unclear, especially in light of General V.K. Singh disowning it in 2010.

These examples indicate an important trend in relation to political involvement and governmental support at the highest level for military change. The government clearly had little hesitation in supporting the organisational restructuring of the army; however, its ability to take the lead and support strategic shifts indicates a much more complex reality. The lead for such changes has been taken by the army, given the specialisation it envisages. However, the success of major strategic changes and their efficacy over a period of time hinge on political understanding and support. This seems conspicuous by its absence in case of changes initiated after the 1975 reforms during the period of Brasstacks and thereafter in relation to Cold Start. In case of Brasstacks, the circumstances are peculiar since the support received by Sundarji for implementing the organisational restructuring was unparalleled, yet there seem to have been gaps in defining a strategic vision. It can also be argued that in both cases, the army exceeded its brief and went ahead with implementing strategies on the basis of in-house doctrines, which may not have had governmental sanction. However, it is more likely that the reason for undertaking strategic shifts in isolation is related to the absence of national strategic directions, as also the inherent failure of the three services to evolve joint strategies and doctrines, as a prelude to their respective service specific guidance. In either case, its resultant impact on the ability to manage change remains detrimental. It not only constrains the influence of envisaged changes, it also limits the expected gains of organisational restructuring, since it closely links with strategy as the driving force for any form of major force structuring.

Some of the modernisation plans suggest a system of 'save and raise', which essentially requires adequate savings from within the system to undertake restructuring. From a political perspective, this approach is practical since it ensures a ceiling on military expenditure. However, it runs the risk of stunted restructuring. It would be a better approach to outline capability objectives and achieve these in stages within existing financial constraints, since this reflects the balance between ends and capacities.

Evidently, political support for military change cannot be taken for granted. The case studies indicate, especially with relation to the post 1975 reforms, that it is equally important for the military leadership to have the ability to win the trust and support of political leaders through a realistic assessment of major changes and its implications on the defence preparedness of the country.

Visionary and Committed Military Leadership

In the absence of desirables like specialist political leaders and bureaucracy, the onus of providing professional direction for long-term military planning rests with the three services. This as per existing literature remains the case, to the extent that "operational directives are usually drafted in Service headquarters. They then go to the ministry for vetting, and are grandiosely issued as Defence Minister's operational directives to the Services".[37]

The case studies reflect on military changes in this regard. While visionary military leadership was evident in case of the changes post 1975, the 1962 changes, despite having a more limited scope of creating defensive deterrence, remained constrained by the army preparing to fight the previous war.[38] It clearly illustrates that making incremental structural changes is not difficult. However, the ability to combine such changes with intellectual vision and commitment, in order to create a paradigm shift for successful war fighting is a challenge. Leaders like Sundarji not only provided visionary leadership, but also were committed to the changes envisaged and created a class of middle-rung commanders, who rose in the hierarchy to take forward the momentum.

This raises the issue of the organisation's ability to throw up visionary leadership. The system seems to be impacted adversely by a number of factors. *First*, the professional military education (PME) system existing in the army is constrained in its ability to groom leaders with the capacity to function as strategic commanders. The system consistently fails to transform many brilliant tactical commanders into operational and strategic visionaries.[39] This is essentially because of the tactical orientation of instruction during formal teaching, focus on rote learning rather than holistic understanding of issues and a very weak theoretical framework to enable understanding of issues beyond the limited scope of military experience. Harsh V. Pant attempts to identify the aim of PME and its relevance in the Indian context:

> The aims of modern PME should be to: develop the military officers' knowledge and understanding of defence in the modern world; demand critical engagement with current research and advanced scholarship on defence and its relationship with the fields of international relations, security studies, military history, war studies and operational experience; encourage a systematic and reflective understanding of contemporary conflicts and the issues surrounding them; promote initiative, originality, creativity and independence of thought in identifying, researching, judging and solving fundamental intellectual problems in this area of study, and develop relevant, transferable skills, especially communication, use of information technology and organisation and management of the learning process. Indian PME lacks every single one of these dimensions.[40]

The post-1962 scenario can be attributed to the limited experience of the senior army hierarchy and the early evolutionary stage of operating in a combined arms environment. In contrast, the reforms post-1975, were facilitated by self-taught leaders like Sundarji.[41] However, the overall limitations in PME are bound to reflect on the future ability of leaders to provide direction through organisational changes.

Second, besides the limitations of PME, the lack of opportunity and exposure in the policy framing environment constrains the strategic outlook of the senior army leadership. This stems from the failure to adequately integrate officers within the structure of the Ministry of Defence (MoD) and the national security institutions.[42] It results in limited exposure to the policy formulation process at the national level, even though they may be posted in the army headquarters. This in turn impinges on their decision-making ability, which is exposed when they finally take up senior positions as Principal Staff Officers, Army Commanders, Vice-Chiefs and Chiefs of Army Staff. This limitation is further accentuated by the short tenure of officers in their appointments, which constrains their ability to understand complex policy framework procedures especially those related to procurements. Hasnain notes, "Simply put, if an officer spends 33 years below general rank, it obviously leaves him six to seven years to contribute at the senior ranks where he commands for short periods and assumes very high responsibility in an unacceptably short time, leaving inexperienced officers and staff at higher ranks."[43]

Third, conversely, since the army brass is not an integral part of the policy planning process in the MoD, it also affects the ministry's ability to take considered decisions on military matters including organisational changes, given the limited exposure of the bureaucracy to service issues. As a result, "there is no established political lobby arguing for change and reform", leaving the emergence of the process from the military establishment itself.[44]

Strong Institutional Structures

The process of developing a long-term strategic assessment is in large measure dependent on the structural strength of the institutions in an organisation. While visionary leadership is an ideal requirement, as is specialised bureaucracy and political leadership, however, these are conditions that cannot be guaranteed. Instead, institution building can guarantee a high order of capability to the organisations, which in turn are responsible for doing the spadework for structural changes and policy formulation. The Indian national security architecture has delivered in times of crisis, as was the case during the 1971 Indo-Pak War and 1999 Kargil conflict. However, the failure to fully institutionalise these procedures, remains a glaring weakness in the institutional capacity building process. Despite a National Security Council and its affiliated set-up being in place, institutional capacities that can provide national strategic and security guidance continue to remain limited. Since this is envisaged as a policy formulation and coordinating body along with its affiliated secretariat, its efficacy, efficiency and effectiveness become the basis for national security guidance. It also ensures systematic and periodic review of guidelines, which in turn become the basis for analysing and planning military change. These limitations are not only visible at the apex level, but also at subsequent stages, especially where agencies are required to function in coordination with others.

In the past, the JIC's weaknesses have been identified. Similarly, the inability of the services to function as integrated and joint organisations has also been witnessed. The weakness of the office of the Chairman Chiefs of Staff Committee is well documented.[45] Besides these joint institutions, the army has also failed to create a strong institutional mechanism as part of its intelligence, training and perspective planning function.[46] This affects the staff work required for developing a strategic vision, and as a result, organisational changes.

The failure to carry out joint assessment, planning and implementation of changes is evident clearly in case of changes after 1962. While this problem was not as acute after 1975, yet its manifestation is conspicuous.[47] Given that even the existing levels of integration are inadequate, this clearly highlights the deeply entrenched propensity of the three services to zealously guard their domains and function within their service specific confines.[48] The army's endeavour to undertake transformation as indicated by the former Chief of the Army Staff, Gen. V.K. Singh, yet again seems to be a single service endeavour, which in the present day and age cannot result in either efficiency or effectiveness, without joint planning and execution.[49]

The process of service specific functioning is saddled with the crippling inability to arbitrate on differences between the three services, affecting the decision-making, which is done by consensus.[50] This is not the most efficient way forward, given the limited understanding of the political elite on such issues and the eventuality of the generalist bureaucracy acting as the arbiter. The absence of the Defence Minister's Committee, a formal forum for resolving professional issues, accentuates this anomaly. At times this has led to issues related to the three services being raised to the level of the NSA or even the Prime Minister's office, a situation that does not bode well for any form of restructuring.

Follow-up Action

Organisational changes are often part of a long-term plan and take time to fructify. In order to achieve optimum efficiency, they also need to be suitably wedded with doctrinal concepts and technological infusion. This implies that the process has to be guided by a series of leaders as part of the army's top brass to take these changes to their intended state of effectiveness. This was visualised in case of the 1975 reforms, wherein the vision to implement changes till 2000 was commenced by Krishna Rao and carried forth by his successors. Even in this case, changes were stalled as a result of limited funding in the nineties, which affected implementation of matching mobility to support echelons of the mechanised forces. In contrast, mountain divisions failed to evolve over the years, as a result of which they reached a state of limited effectiveness over a period of time.[51]

Follow-up action is not merely associated with the army. It is also critical to ensure that infrastructural limitations are simultaneously addressed to ensure that military changes can be effective. The changes post-1962 were not accompanied by the creation of requisite infrastructure along the border with China. The limitations in this regard continue to remain a challenge, even after five decades, wherein the existing road communication network and aviation support assets lag behind the force capabilities of the army.

A similar limitation exists in terms of the ability of the army and its support institutions to develop indigenous capabilities to facilitate military change, as a follow-up of organisational restructuring. The Indian Navy has displayed this capability through its design bureau, which has provided direction to the process of ship building. It is time for similar institutional capacities to be created within the army and the tri-services environment.

NOTES

1. See *Annual Report: 1963-64*, Ministry of Defence, New Delhi, p. 2.
2. See Jawaharlal Nehru, "February 2, 1962", in G Parthasarthi (Ed), *Letters to Chief Ministers: 1947-1964, Vol 5 1958-1964*, Oxford University Press, Delhi, 1989, p. 573.

3. Ibid., p. 596.
4. John Kenneth Galbraith, *Ambassador's Journal*, Hamish Hamilton, London, 1969, p. 434.
5. K. Alan Kronstadt, "Pakistan-U.S. Relations", *CRS Issue Brief for Congress*, May 14, 2004, at http://fpc.state.gov/documents/organization/32840.pdf (Accessed April 28, 2015).
6. For a detailed account of India's defence purchases from the former Soviet Union, see P. R. Chari, "Indo-Soviet Military Cooperation: A Review", *Asian Survey*, 19 (3), March 1979, pp. 230-244, at http://www.jstor.org/stable/2643691 (Accessed April 28, 2015).
7. Feroze Hassan Khan, *Eating Grass: The Making of the Pakistani Bomb*, Foundation Books, New Delhi, 2013, p. 126.
8. General K. V. Krishna Rao, *Prepare or Perish: A Study of National Security*, Lancer Publishers, New Delhi, 1991, p. 400.
9. Ibid., p. 406.
10. Ibid.
11. An interview with Lt Gen. Satish Nambiar, New Delhi, November 3, 2014.
12. "BMP-2", Weapons and Warfare, at http://weaponsandwarfare.com/?p=5249.
13. Ali Ahmed, *India's Doctrine Puzzle: Limiting War in South Asia*, Routledge, New Delhi, 2014, pp. 41-45.
14. Ibid.8, pp 38-39.
15. Ali Ahmed, "Strategic Culture and Indian Self Assurance", *Journal of Peace Studies*, 17 (2/3), April-September 2010, at http://www.icpsnet.org/adm/pdf/1291710631.pdf (Accessed Aug 12, 2015).
16. Ibid. Ali Ahmed relates the shift to three factors, which include economic advances, political culture which led to a nationalist conservative outlook and movement in conventional and nuclear doctrines.
17. David Alexander, "India and U.S. Agree on Ground-breaking Defense Projects", Reuters, June 3, 2015, at http://www.reuters.com/article/us-india-usa-idUSKBN0OJ1NX20150603 (Accessed on March 17, 2016).
18. Theo Farrell and Terry Terriff (eds.), *The Sources of Military Change: Culture, Politics, Technology*, Lynne Rienner Publishers, Boulder, 2002, p. 6.
19. Ibid.
20. Terry Terriff, "U.S. Ideas and Military Change in NATO, 1989-1994", in Theo Farrell and Terry Terriff (eds.), *The Sources of Military Change: Culture, Politics, Technology*, Lynne Rienner Publishers, Boulder, 2002, pp. 92-94.
21. Stephen Cohen, *India: Emerging Power*, Oxford University Press, New Delhi, 2002, pp. 63-64. The author highlights the consensus amongst India's strategic community about its being a status quo power. He attributes a part of this to India's inability to change the status quo.
22. Based on the author's experience, all these terms mentioned are an integral part of defence planning at most levels of planning in the army and have become inherent to operational discussions.
23. K. Subrahmanyam, "The Making of a Security Policy Structure", in K. Subrahmanyam and Arthur Monteiro, *Shedding Shibboleths: India's Evolving Strategic Outlook*, Wordsmiths, Delhi, 2005, p. 20.
24. Maj. Gen. D.K. Palit, *War in the High Himalayas*, Lancer International, New Delhi, 1991, pp. 85 and 176.
25. K. Subrahmanyam, "Revamping Intelligence", in K. Subrahmanyam and Arthur Monteiro, *Shedding Shibboleths: India's Evolving Strategic Outlook*, Wordsmiths, Delhi, 2005, p. 74.
26. *A Case for Intelligence Reforms in India: IDSA Task Force Report*, Institute for Defence Studies

and Analyses (IDSA), New Delhi, 2012, p. 67.

27. Ibid., p. 68.
28. Gen. J. N. Chaudhari, "India's Problems of National Security in the Seventies", USI National Security Lectures, United Service Institution of India, 1971, p. 12.
29. Lt Gen. Vijay Oberoi, "Need for Holistic Restructuring of the Indian Military", *Journal of Defence Studies*, 2 (1), Summer 2008, at http://www.idsa.in/jds/2_1_2008_NeedforHolisticRestructuringoftheIndianMilitary_VOberoi.html (Accessed March 30, 2015).
30. "Former PM Rajiv Gandhi Was in Dark about Brasstacks Operations", *Deccan Chronicle*, August 03, 2014, at http://www.deccanchronicle.com/140803/nation-current-affairs/article/former-pm-rajiv-gandhi-was-dark-about-brasstacks-operation (Accessed April 29, 2015).
31. Gen. Deepak Kapoor (Retd), "Role of Private Sector in Defence", *India Strategic*, October 2013, at http://www.indiastrategic.in/topstories3061_Role_private_sector_in_defence.htm (Accessed April 29, 2015).
32. R.D. Pradhan, *Debacle to Resurgence: Y.B. Chavan Defence Minister (1962-1966)*, Atlantic Publishers, New Delhi, 2013, p. 21.
33. Ibid. The author devotes a chapter each to Chavan's visits to the three countries in a bid to buy weapons for the three services.
34. The establishment of ordnance factories to include the one at Avadi are examples of this effort.
35. "Now, Mani Shankar Aiyar Says Rajiv Gandhi Was in Dark about Exercise Brasstacks", *The Times of India*, August 3, 2014, at http://timesofindia.indiatimes.com/india/Now-Mani-Shankar-Aiyar-says-Rajiv-Gandhi-was-in-dark-about-Operation-Brasstacks/articleshow/39510383.cms (Accessed August 11, 2015).
36. Pinaki Bhattacharya, "Army and IAF Face off over New War Plan", *Mail Today*, December 14, 2009, at http://indiatoday.intoday.in/story/Army+and+IAF+face+off+over+new+ war+plan/1/74898.html (Accessed August 11, 2015).
37. K. Subrahmanyam, "Does India Have a Strategic Perspective?", in K. Subrahmanyam and Arthur Monteiro, *Shedding Shibboleths: India's Evolving Strategic Outlook*, Wordsmiths, New Delhi, 2005, p. 9.
38. The army's outlook was constrained by the inability integrate closely with the other services, follow an attrition mindset, failure to adapt to mobile warfare, improve command, control and intelligence functions.
39. See K. Subrahmanyam, "Structure and Personnel Policy of the Armed Forces", in K. Subrahmanyam and Arthur Monteiro, *Shedding Shibboleths: India's Evolving Strategic Outlook*, Wordsmiths, New Delhi, 2005, pp. 64-65.
40. Harsh V. Pant, "Bridging the Soldier-Scholar Divide", *The Hindu*, June 4, 2013, at http://www.thehindu.com/todays-paper/tp-opinion/bridging-the-soldierscholar-divide/article4779787.ece (Accessed March 26, 2015).
41. Sundarji was not only an architect of India's mechanisation and concepts of modern warfare, he is also attributed with contributing significantly to India's nuclear doctrine. See K Subrahmanyan, No. 37, p. 8.
42. Lt Gen. S. K. Sinha, "Higher Defence Organisation", USI National Security Lecture - 1990, United Service Institution of India, New Delhi, 1991, p. 33.
43. Lt Gen. Syed Ata Hasnain, "Why the Indian Army Isn't a Lethal War Machine Today", *Daily O*, January 15, 2015, at http://www.dailyo.in/politics/why-the-indian-army-isnt-a-lethal-war-machine-today-army-day-infrastructure/story/1/1512.html (Accessed March 30, 2015).
44. See Stephen P. Cohen and Sunil Dasgupta, *Arming without Aiming: India's Military*

Modernization, Viking, New Delhi, 2010, p. 69.

45. See Air Chief Marshal P. C. Lal (Retd), "Some Problems of Defence", United Service Institution of India, New Delhi, 1977, pp. 74-75.
46. The failure is marked by short tenures of officers, their generic background and inadequate specialisation and the limited mandate of military intelligence.
47. See Stephen P. Cohen and Sunil Dasgupta, No. 44, p. 43.
48. Lt Gen. Vijay Oberoi relates it to the resistance amongst the services to let go of their "fiefdoms". See Lt Gen. Vijay Oberoi, No. 29.
49. Gen. V. K. Singh, "Army Must Set an Example: New Army Chief to NDTV", An Interview, NDTV, April 1, 2010, at http://www.ndtv.com/india-news/army-must-set-an-example-new-chief-to-ndtv-414148 (Accessed March 26, 2015).
50. See Kapil Kak, "Direction of Higher Defence – II", IDSA, at http://www.idsa-india.org/an-jul8-1.html (Accessed April 15, 2015).
51. Brig. Rumel Dahiya, "Modernisation of Infantry in India", *Journal of Defence Studies,* 4 (3), 2010, pp. 137 and 144.

PART II

Military Change in Counterinsurgency

ADAPTATION TO CHANGE

The fast-evolving nature of threats and warfare forces change and adaptation. In the context of conventional threats, change is often associated with shifts which are a complete break from the past. This leads to major transformations in the war fighting methods. These changes are also a product of concepts, implemented through superior strategy and exploitation of available technology. It challenges straightjacketed thinking and transforms armies through proactive measures.

A brief assessment of Indian history is revealing in this regard. Babur's employment of field artillery was instrumental in defeating a much larger army led by Ibrahim Lodi. As the battle progressed, the shock action created by artillery, in conjunction with the employment of matchlocks, cavalry and superior tactics carried the day and laid the foundation of the Mughal dynasty in India.[1] The Indian victory during the 1971 War in East Pakistan (now Bangladesh), is yet another example of superior strategy. The fortress defensive system built around important communication centres was rendered ineffectual, by bypassing these and hitting at the nerve centre at Dacca. Classical manoeuvre warfare outclassed the Pakistani Army's preparation for an attrition battle through a lightening campaign.[2]

In contrast, counterinsurgency (CI) operations present a contradiction for a conventional army and other security forces. The duration of the conflict is characterised by its prolonged nature of operations, often to the advantage of the insurgents, aiming to defeat a superior force by attrition and breaking the will of the state to fight. The relative technological dumbing down of a CI conflict in contrast to a high technology modern battlefield takes away the inherent advantage from state forces. The induction of the army in an area with hostile population and more often than not negligible intelligence keeps it off balance and reactive. This forces the army to adapt to these circumstances, which change with every CI campaign, minimise its casualties and create conditions conducive for effective governance. The nature of conflicts in CI operations present a steep learning curve for an organisation like the army, which is organised, equipped and primarily trained for conventional warfare and has a distinct discomfiture for CI, especially against its own people.

The Indian Army has been involved almost continuously in CI operations since 1955. During more than these six decades, despite a number of challenges, the army has made a commendable contribution towards national security. However, very often, lost in the resolution of some of these conflicts and attrition ratios of others, are invaluable lessons of the army's adaptation to evolving challenges and managing change.

This section will evaluate the army's ability to adapt to threats and evolving conditions in CI operations, with an aim of highlighting the strengths and more importantly its weaknesses. It undertakes a detailed assessment of the Indian Army's adaptation to military change in the context of CI operations by analysing change at the strategic, organisational and operational level.

It is argued and illustrated that in contrast to military change in conventional wars which is brought about when armies adopt an approach that is often revolutionary, driven by cutting-edge technology, directed from the highest level, making it essentially top-down; in CI operations, this process is evolutionary, with relatively limited influence of technology. More often than not it is based on bottom-up adaptation, even if in some cases it manifests in top-down implementation.

The section is based on a brief analysis of 27 case studies. These are not the only instances of military change in CI operations. However, given the large cross section of examples examined over an extended period of time, as well as geographical spread, including some from the pre-independence period, the sample provides an objective basis for empirical evidence on military change (**See Annexure 1**). Each case has been analysed for the following:

- What has been the type of military change in CI operations in India?
- Has the change been top-down, or bottom-up?
- Was the change major or limited?
- What were the drivers for military change?
- What was its impact?

NOTES

1. Paul K. Davis, *100 Decisive Battles: From Ancient Times to Present*, Oxford University Press, New York, 2001, pp. 182-184.
2. For a first-hand account of the War, see: Maj. Gen. Lachhman Singh, *Victory in Bangladesh*, Natraj Publications, Dehradun, 2005; Maj. Gen. Sukhwant Singh, *Liberation of Bangladesh*, Lancer International, New Delhi, 1980; Maj. Gen. D. K. Palit, *Lighting Campaign: The India-Pakistan War 1971*, Lancers Publishers, New Delhi, 1997.

5

Change in Military Strategy

Counterinsurgency (CI) operations in India are often referred to as sub-conventional operations. This is primarily because of the wide range of operations below the threshold of conventional state on state wars that the Indian Army has had to contend with over the years. This is not only relevant to the army in the post-independence period, but also prior to it. During this phase, the British Indian Army undertook a number of expeditionary forays into the subcontinent, and at times beyond it to suppress warring tribes in a bid to ensure that its writ ran in these areas. These experiences have been documented by officers from the period and throw light on the nature of these operations. In many ways, the conduct of CI operations undertaken by the army post-independence were a continuation of operations in the sub-conventional domain, though with very distinct and relevant changes that characterised them. This chapter attempts to identify some of these relevant changes from the perspective of military strategy. In doing so, the period of approximately a century indicates an interesting timeline of evolutionary trends, which were dictated by a number of factors in the form of drivers and shapers of these shifts.

Frontier Warfare

The Indian Army has long years of experience in CI operations. Prior to 1947, in the pre-independence period, the British Indian Army operated against tribal warriors in the North West Frontier Province (NWFP; now in Pakistan), areas of Afghanistan, Nagaland and Mizoram. Given the unique conditions of each of these phases, the army adapted to the varying complexion of threats posed in each theatre of conflict.

Amongst these initial forays, the challenge posed by the Afghan warriors in the NWFP was possibly amongst the bloodiest series of sub-conventional campaigns fought by the army. These campaigns witnessed an elusive adversary, with the ability to carry out sharp attacks, followed by equally quick retreats. The challenge forced the British Indian Army to adapt to these realities and prompted the inclusion of this kind of warfare into existing literature for the officer corps of the army. The lessons on frontier warfare were incorporated in the *Field Service Regulations: Part I Operations, 1909.*[1] The chapter dedicated to frontier warfare refers to the adversary as, "Warfare against an Uncivilised Enemy". It goes on to highlight the importance of forcing the enemy to offer "organised resistance", and recommends a number of ways to achieve this. One of these suggests:

> Should the enemy refuse to make an organised resistance, the occupation of his country, the seizure of his flocks and supplies, and the destruction of his villages and crops may be necessary to obtain his submission.

In 1932, General Sir Andrew Skeen's book, *Passing it On: Fighting the Pashtun on Afghanistan's Frontier*, was first published. It was addressed to the "junior officer of the infantry", with an aim of educating him about the nature of adversary and warfare based on the author's rich experience.[2] Skeen reinforced the *1909 Regulations* and emphasised the need to bring the Pathan tribesmen to combat and undertake extreme punitive reprisal. He writes: "... Unless the enemy is completely crushed, he will rally to defend his property or revenge loss, and you will find him fully as fierce as a wasp in a harried hive."[3]

This strategy required a major shift from the more conventional approach against standing armies, wherein battles were fought in the Indian subcontinent, with forces arraigned against each other.The British Indian Army aimed to militarily subdue the area by punitive expeditionary operations. The military strategy was formulated based on the lessons from tactical operations and intimate understanding of the adversary. It was the culmination of the cumulative learning of officers and men alike under difficult conditions. The ground-up tactical adaptation eventually led to the major step of release of the field service regulations, as well as Skeen's book, which successfully guided the conduct of operations thereafter.

A similar approach to operations was evident in Northeast India in the pre-independence period. The 1889-90 expedition witnessed a severe reprisal by the British, as a result of repeated Lushai raids and killings. Subir Bhaumik quotes the report of the Chief Commissioner of Chittagong, W.S. Oldham: "All villages, except Aitur and Malthuna in North Lushai Hills, were ruled by widows."[4]

The impact of these methods on the officers and men of the army was bound to have a residual influence, which is borne by Skeen's book being a part of recommended reading for officers in the Indian Army, at least till 1965.[5]

CI Operations in the Mid-fifties and Early Sixties

The political mandate prior to independence along the country's periphery aimed at suppressing violent tribes and maintenance of a degree of order, even as the locals were allowed to undertake autonomous socio-economic activities.[6] The army ensured security of British-controlled areas in vicinity of such regions and treated some of these as buffer states. This led to occasional expeditionary operations to achieve these objectives.[7] While the British colonial rule was guided by its own interests, which in turn defined its strategy, independent India's political and military leaders were faced with major challenges in order to redefine the military direction for sub conventional operations.

First, the Indian Army was oriented towards conventional threats and operations. The experience during the Second World War, and thereafter, for nearly half a decade, saw the army organise, equip, train and operate against conventional armies. While this witnessed its evolution into a first-rate army for such operations, it gained little experience against sub-conventional threats. Moreover, the army's limited past experience as part of frontier operations, which laid the foundation for CI operations, was not enough for fighting an insurgency in a newly independent democratic country.

Second, operational challenges were compounded by the lack of experience of the governing elite and senior hierarchy of the army in dealing with CI operations. This specifically included issues like higher defence management, security management and clarity on dealing with internal threats. CI operations required clear politico-military vision, maturity and patience from political leaders, along with the ability to provide a clear mandate to the army.

Third, the army's organisation, especially at the battalion level, which represents the cutting edge of CI operations, was not suited for such responsibilities, as it had been tailored for conventional threats of the kind faced during the Second World War. Constraints included a large number of men being tied down with heavy calibre weapon systems, which was not conducive for CI operations. However, since the primary responsibility of the army remained external threats, the possibility of making changes to the organisation of a battalion, specifically for CI operations, presented a difficult challenge.

Fourth, the army's forays into CI operations also brought forth the challenge of legal sanction for its deployment and operations. The existing laws gave these powers only to the police. However, the nature of responsibility of the army required a change in the laws to facilitate its deployment.

The political component of these challenges was factored by the national leadership while dealing with insurgencies. This reflected in their mature understanding of the threat and resultant guidance provided to the army. The army's approach was defined by this direction, as well as the nature of threat it faced. This led to tempering of the operational military approach with a clear political mandate.

The very first step required the reversal of politico-military objectives under British India. Prime Minister Nehru issued a political directive to the army deployed to secure areas dominated by Naga tribals, the first ethnic group to take up arms.[8] One of Nehru's biographers, Sarvepalli Gopal, notes:

> But the military approach, while necessary, was not adequate; and Nehru insisted that soldiers and officials should always remember that the Nagas were fellow-countrymen, who were not merely to be suppressed but, at some stage had to be won over.[9]

This approach was a major departure from the erstwhile British policy of expeditionary military forays into the region and required the army to recalibrate its response.

The basis for the army's doctrinal direction can be found in the Order of the Day issued by the then Chief of Army Staff to the troops being deployed for operations in Nagaland in 1956. It read:

> You are not there to fight the people in the area, but to protect them. You are fighting only those who threaten the people and who are a danger to the lives and properties of the people.[10]

It was these clear guidelines which laid the foundation for the army's military response. It is therefore not surprising that there was a distinct difference between the pre- and post- independence period, in terms of the nature of operations conducted.

While these guidelines provided the necessary political and military direction, however, given the army's negligible experience in CI operations until then, these continued to be influenced by conventional operations. In the context of Mizoram, Lt Gen. Mathew Thomas notes:

> We had to open all axes from south to north and had to clear all the major villages along the central route. In doing that, people were alienated, to a certain extent, due to the fact that we were not very sure about how to go about things. None of the battalions that were from 61 Mountain Brigade had any experience of counter insurgency .[11]

Until the mid-sixties, the army's doctrinal orientation was characterised by "search and clear" operations, without holding areas, which were frequented by the guerrillas. Bodies of troops were stationed at selective locations, with the direction to operate over long distances in substantial numbers, thereby reinforcing the writ of the state. The role of the army was focused on such military operations, with limited time and resources invested for winning over the population and establishing a broad-based intelligence network. Lt Col. S.P. Anand highlights the nature of search and clear operations undertaken during the period: "These patrols remain in these areas for weeks and depend on para-drops for their supplies."[12]

It is evident from the army's involvement during this period that the shift in strategic direction was initiated as a top-down process, from the highest echelons of civil and military decision-making. This strategic guidance was a major departure from the erstwhile policy followed prior to independence. It was necessitated by the nature of sub-conventional operational challenge, which required a calibrated response. The strategic guidance also became the basis for the military strategy of the army for CI operations, with an attempt to tailor it to prevalent challenges. The strategy succeeded in reorienting the army; however, limitations of numbers, a sustained influence of conventional operations and lack of training continued to limit its CI capability.[13]

CI Operations from Mid-sixties till the Seventies

The second phase of strategic change was initially influenced by British operations in Malaya and other communist guerrilla movements during the period. This involved adoption of a rudimentary 'clear and hold' strategy, which involved deployment of the army in a CI grid in affected areas.

The conduct of 'clear and hold'[14] strategy by the army also saw the implementation of the concept of "protected villages". The grouping of villages was an attempt at adapting to the challenge of insurgents drawing their sustenance from the local population. The strategy required greater numbers to establish physical presence of the army; however, purely from a military perspective, the grouping of villages facilitated the process in terms of provision of security to the local population and keeping them isolated from the terrorists. The protected villages concept was based on the experience of the British Army in the Malaya insurgency. Lt Col. S.P. Anand, writing in the United Service Institution of India (USI)'s 1971 *USI Journal*, reinforced this thinking: "...The pattern followed was the one proposed and practised by Gen. Briggs in Malaya." He describes this as:

(a) Cut the insurgents off from the population which supports them.
(b) Make the zones in which the underground move untenable.
(c) Act simultaneously over a wide expanse for a long period of time, to wear out the insurgents.[15]

The logic of isolating the population from the insurgents was well-reasoned; however, the means adopted were not conducive to winning them over, and alienated the people.

As part of this initiative, groups of villages were patrolled by the army, duly assisted by the Central Reserve Police battalions. The policy suffered from a lack of understanding of the local customs and culture. For example, the local people subsisted on shifting cultivation, and by bringing them together in artificial colonies, without the requisite job opportunities, the locals were potentially made dependent on government support for subsistence.[16] They were also alienated from their traditional way of life, which caused deep resentment over a period of time.[17] The fact that the government and the army did not resort to this practice after the Mizo CI operations reinforces the inadequacy of the experience, despite achieving eventual success in the CI efforts in the state.

Brig. (later Lt Gen.) S.K. Sinha, writing in the *USI Journal* in 1970, gives an indication of the Indian Army's thought process during the period. He suggests measures to include: projection of an "alternative ideal"; "grouping of local population" in order to prevent local support; "dilution of population" by outside settlements along with the Chinese example of Tibet; and "sound development plans" for environmental improvement.[18] He goes on to reinforce the need for an integrated civil and military organisation on the lines of the Malaya model.

Sinha also discarded the notion of minimum force as applied in case of aid to civil authorities, when he wrote: "At the end of the scale is the mistaken notion that the Army should conduct counter insurgency operations as aid to the civil power. This is a totally unrealistic concept. The technique of dispersal of unlawful assemblies with minimum force cannot be applied to warfare of this type."[19] While Sinha correctly distinguishes between dispersing a mob to help civil authorities and CI, however, the redundancy of the principle of minimum force, as indicated by him was flawed, as is evident from later doctrinal shifts. The task of domination of the area was reinforced through a "grid" system of deployment,[20] as was the emphasis on the conduct of security forces. Sinha wrote, "The conduct of Security Forces towards the locals must be exemplary at all times. Any attempt to harass, torture or otherwise maltreat the people must be ruthlessly stopped."[21] Despite this clear understanding of the importance of winning over of the population, options like "imposing of food rationing" as executed in Malaya, was reflective of inadequate understanding of the implementation of the "Winning Hearts and Minds" (WHAM) measures.

This period witnessed a strategic shift, which aimed to partly correct the bias towards conventional operations. The establishment of a CI grid and the clear and hold strategy thus became the linchpin of operations. The shift was a result of lessons learnt during the first decade and British experience in Malaya. The change was a major shift from the earlier approach to operations, as was its impact. The evolutionary changes in the conduct of operations and the lessons learnt therein created a bottom-up capillary action, which eventually drove the top-down clear and hold strategy. These changes were also influenced by environmental pressure, which emanated from people's rejection of policies like protected villages.

This period also eventually witnessed the opening of the first CI school at Veirangte in 1970. It provided systematic training based on experiences in the CI environment. Even as this change was top-down in its concept and implementation, the inputs and lessons were provided by case studies of infantry battalions operating in the area. It was a major change, from localised on the job training to a systematic approach, which took into account a holistic view of insurgent tactics and CI operations.

Iron Fist and Velvet Glove Strategy

The limitations noticed during the initial period of adapting to change were corrected by the army over a period of time. This was a result of lessons learnt at the tactical level, as part of the evolutionary process, and also due to increasing pressure by human rights groups, local population and the media.[22]

The release of the army's sub-conventional doctrine might suggest the promulgation of the strategy in 2006; however, these changes did not commence with its formal enunciation. A number of individual changes were already in place since the mid-nineties. These did receive an impetus with declaration of the formal doctrine and became better defined thereafter. These collective changes led to an even balance between military operations and WHAM. The *Doctrine for Sub Conventional Operations (DSCO)* highlights this aspect in its overarching theme:

> Since the centre of gravity for such operations is the populace, operations have to be undertaken with full respect to Human Rights and in accordance with the laws of the land ... This underscores the importance of people friendly operations that are conducted with a civil face.[23]

This balance is best described by the "Iron Fist with Velvet Glove" strategy. Gen. J.J. Singh, former Chief of the Army Staff, coined the term to illustrate the underlying theme of the doctrine. He said:

> ... I have emphasised the concept of 'Iron Fist with Velvet Glove', which implies a humane approach towards the populace at large in the conflict zone. This also implies the use of overwhelming force only against foreign terrorists and other hardcore inimical elements, while affording full opportunity to indigenous misguided elements to shun violence and join the mainstream.[24]

The army leadership reinforced that insurgencies are a violent expression of political problems. Therefore, solutions must also pursue a political trajectory.[25] This acceptance of the nature of threat, further defined the response, which rather than merely focussing on the insurgent, preferred to target the insurgency.

The erstwhile limitation of the bias towards conventional operations was also addressed by reinforcing the need to reorient commanders and men towards CI operations. The *DSCO* highlights this aspect by emphasising on the protracted duration of operations, changed rules of engagement, requirement of multi-agency integrated operations, the challenge of fighting one's own people and criticality of people friendly operations.[26] It further emphasises the need for specialised training to imbibe these facets prior to induction for training.

The grid system of deployment was formalised from the mid-nineties, and it ensured security of population centres, lines of communication and critical infrastructure.[27] In addition, the threat of proxy war across the Line of Control (LoC) was simultaneously addressed through deployment aimed at controlling both infiltration and exfiltration. This in areas like Jammu and Kashmir (J&K), because a part of the three-tier deployment, with the army at the LoC, Rashtriya Rifles (RR) battalions in the hinterland and central police organisations along with local police in urban population centres. This strengthened local governance by involving the police in day-to-day law and order duties, even as areas more prone to terrorism were controlled by RR. Evidence of the army's intent to stay away from urban areas and policing duties was seen during protracted street protests in Kashmir valley in 2010. This resulted in over 100 fatal casualties; however, over a period of time, the local and central police units developed the necessary capability and skills to control such incidents of mass frenzy.[28]

There was also greater emphasis on clinical operations on the basis of specific intelligence in the *DSCO*: "To obviate inconvenience to the populace, operations should be based on hard intelligence rather than being conducted on prophylactic basis."[29] Small team operations received a fillip. It potentially increased the chances of contact with terrorists. This was envisaged along with the capability and flexibility of grouping and regrouping of forces.

Perception management received special attention with emphasis on areas where the army was deployed for CI operations. Existing headquarters were restructured by providing additional staff for these specialised functions. These organisational changes were accompanied by efforts to change the method of operations which aimed to limit the negative impact of collateral damage and prolonged presence of the army in populated areas.[30]

The changes were essentially part of the army's military strategy; however, these also formed a part of the larger politico-military strategy of the government. It was brought about not only as a result of the emerging threats, but also due to the demand for greater transparency, accountability and compliance with human rights while conducting operations. This was accompanied by the understanding within the army that respect for human rights facilitated rather than detracted from the successful conduct of operations. It also led to improvement of human intelligence, with the local population displaying greater cooperation with the army. This top-down approach was influenced by years of experience at the tactical level and succeeded in creating a major change in the army's approach to CI operations.

These changes over a period of time provided certain common guidelines for the conduct of CI operations.

First, there was broad-based consensus that domestic insurgents are misguided citizens of the country, who need be brought back into the national mainstream. This called for a different approach vis-à-vis foreign terrorists, who were and remain an instrument of Pakistani proxy war against India. While the former have chosen to surrender in large numbers, the latter remain intent on undertaking sensational acts of terrorism, which can only be stopped by their neutralisation.[31]

Second, the approach to domestic insurgency was marked by willingness to undertake political negotiations, which in more cases than one involved devolution of greater socio-economic and political autonomy. The only stipulation was the exploration of solutions within the parameters of a united India. The record of past negotiations indicates that the government has gone as far as amending the constitution on a number of occasions.[32]

Third, the Indian approach was characterised by the desire to utilise minimum force while undertaking operations against insurgents. It is for this reason that the use of heavy calibre weapons like artillery and mortars, helicopter gunships, aircraft and drones equipped with standoff missiles was discouraged and has attained a hands-off status for CI operations.[33]

Fourth, unlike a number of developed countries, where the pressure of time severely impacted the direction of a CI campaign, India exploited this vital factor to its advantage. This is influenced in part by the fact that these movements have been fought on Indian soil and not beyond the geographical boundaries. Despite the pressure of increased transparency, accountability and 24/7 scrutiny by the media, the army has been able to fight insurgents over long durations, without any adverse impact on its ability to motivate soldiers. This, as events suggest, has more often than not forced a number of adversaries to the negotiating table. A brief analysis of 12 militant movements across the country provides evidence to support this observation as seen till 2014.[34] Of the 12 instances analysed, six resolved insurgencies lasted from seven to 26 years, with an average of 16 years. The average duration of the unresolved movements is 37 years. Amongst these, none of the movements were able to achieve their stated objectives and ongoing negotiations suggest a similar trajectory for the balance.

Major Increase in Force Levels

There have been instances after the initial induction of forces in a CI environment that required a major increase in force levels to deal with a worsening situation. This resulted from an underestimation of threat, limited availability of numbers or the expansion of the conflict by terrorist groups. J&K presented a mix of these very challenges. During the initial years of violence in the late eighties and early nineties, the army was also deployed in Sri Lanka, Punjab and some regions of Northeast India. This placed constraints on its ability to release forces for J&K. The succeeding years also witnessed an expansion in threat levels due to the outward flow of terrorist violence, after its initial impact in the Kashmir Valley. The decision to raise RR battalions was not only a major military shift in the organisational pattern of forces, it was an equally important change for rightsizing force levels in J&K. Similarly, the induction of combat divisions during the Kargil conflict of 1999, facilitated in stabilising a worsening situation thereafter. However, some cases of temporary induction of forces were followed by subsequent de-induction, thereby ensuring that only the requisite numbers were maintained in each area of operation.[35]

The change in force levels was a top-down decision, based on the operational threat perception in the area. It was a part of the overall strategy of fighting the CI campaign. As evident from the case of J&K, both induction and de-induction was carried out based on the prevailing security situation in the state, making the change reversible.

Change in Legal Provisions

The existing law of the land in India does not allow the army to search houses, raid suspected areas and arrest people. These powers remain with the police. This was realised soon after the deployment of the army for CI operations in the mid-fifties. It led to framing of laws which when applied to a particular area, allowed the induction of army and simultaneously gave the powers of search, raid and arrest of suspected insurgents and terrorists. The first major law in this regard was called the Armed Forces (Special) Powers Act [AFSPA], 1958.[36] This law was subsequently amended to enlarge its geographical applicability in Northeast India. It was also promulgated in the states of Punjab and Jammu and Kashmir, with minor variations.[37] While the law was framed to facilitate the limited and occasional deployment of the army in CI operations, however, it has been applicable almost continuously since then, given the perceived challenges to internal security.

The law has not witnessed major changes since its promulgation. However, a court case filed by the Naga People's Movement of Human Rights, etc., led the Supreme Court to uphold the constitutional validity of the Act. In addition, it directed binding implementation of Dos and Don'ts issued by the army along with suggested amendments by the Court. The Court ruled:

> The instructions contained in the list of "Dos and Don'ts" shall be suitably amended so as to bring them in conformity with the guidelines contained in the decisions of this Court and to incorporate the safeguards that are contained in clauses (a) to (d) of Section 4 and Section 5 of the Central Act as construed and also the direction contained in the order of this Court dated July 4, 1991 in Civil Appeal No. 2551 of 1991.[38]

Evidently, the change in AFSPA related more to formalising procedures, in an evolutionary process, in terms of the employment of the army, especially since the army was already following the Dos and Don'ts as part of its standard procedures. These changes were therefore, a result of attempts at improving the army's operational procedures and addressing environmental pressure, which demanded greater accountability and transparency. The changes were top-down in nature, given the level at which the amendments were formulated and resulted in better compliance of human rights during operations.

LoC Obstacle System

Amongst the most important strategic decisions taken in the fight against terrorism, especially in the case of J&K, was the establishment of an obstacle system along the LoC. It became operational in 2004 and despite the difficult geographical conditions in J&K, it proved to be an effective system, especially for stopping large-scale infiltration from Pakistan. The fence, surveillance equipment and troops deployed proved to be an effective innovation necessitated by the threat of increasing cross-border infiltration. The obstacle system has been established in close proximity of the LoC at a distance varying from approximately two to four kilometres. In most cases, given the active interference by Pakistan at the time of its erection, the fence was constructed on the home side of the mother ridge. It was reinforced with the help of seismic, infrared and motion sensors, in addition to night-vision devices, radars and physical obstacles.

Dynamic deployment of troops along the LoC fence reinforced this strategic turning point for fighting terrorism in J&K. The period prior to establishment of the fence had witnessed infiltration in large groups, which led to high levels of violence in the affected areas of the state. However, the fence and its associated deployment became instrumental in ensuring control over infiltration on the LoC, even as security forces simultaneously neutralised terrorists in the hinterland. The deployment on the fence consists of a tiered pattern, along with the provision of reserves at every level. Given the difficult geography of the area, a near permanent system of observation, patrolling and ambushes ensures that the obstacle system with its early warning equipment brings in dynamism and limits the possibility of infiltration.

Serious interference from Pakistan notwithstanding, given its resultant effectiveness, the possibility of the fence coming up earlier could potentially have reduced infiltration substantially. Stephen Cohen feels, "Frankly, I am surprised the Indians didn't build it earlier."[39] This change was a top-down decision and was driven by operational threats and shaped by technology, which enhanced its effectiveness.

Use of Local Militia

There have been a number of examples of the use of local militia over the years. It began with the security forces facing stiff resistance from guerrillas in Northeast India. In one such operation, the Inspector General of Police, G.S. Arya was killed in Mizoram. His successor, Brigadier G.S. Randhawa, applied the 'pseudo-gangs' experiment of Kenya to Mizoram.[40] He employed relatives of locals killed for reprisals against Mizo National Front (MNF) insurgents. The experiment was soon stopped, given the inherent lack of control over armed members of the population.

The government attempted this experiment on subsequent occasions as well. While in the short term, it facilitated military operations with the advantage of local knowledge and improved flow of information, however, almost every experiment has subsequently led to poor control and reprisal attacks, alienating the people in the long run. The case of surrendered United Liberation Front of Assam (ULFA) cadres, *Salwa Judum* in Chhattisgarh[41] and the *Ikhwan* in J&K, highlight similar lessons. Though these experiments were initiated by the police,[42] and not by the army, yet given the close operational linkage of some of these groups with the army, this example has relevance to the process of military change. This experiment was an attempt at creating a major shift, which as a result of poor implementation, displayed mixed results. In most cases, what began as a bottom-up initiative, as illustrated in the case of Mizoram, was subsequently employed as a top-down directive as seen in case of *Salwa Judum*, in the face of serious operational threats, with limited success.

Use of Offensive Air Support

The army evolved its operational approach over a period of time in CI operations. In the case of Mizoram, where insurgency broke out in 1966, the shock of MNF cadres taking over Assam Rifles posts saw the government order stern military countermeasures. The series of actions witnessed the employment of air power in punitive role, under what were perceived as exceptional circumstances.[43] However, this innovation in CI operations was an experiment, which was not repeated given the psychological impact it had on the population for years to come.[44] It reflected a negative cost benefit analysis, as a result of the inherent inaccuracy of bombs, limited ability to immediately exploit the shock action and, most importantly, the resultant alienation of the population.[45] Subsequent attempts to employ even helicopters in offensive role have been opposed by the army, despite heavy security forces casualties in Naxal-hit areas of Central India.[46] This top-down major change attempted did not give the desired results, and subsequently, the role of air support has been limited to logistics and support operations in CI operations.

Change in Goals

The strategic goals outlined for the army did not change substantially in most CI-affected areas. This entails the provision of a "secure environment, whereas various institutions of the government can function devoid of any inimical interference".[47] It includes limiting violence and threat to lives and property. There have been two instances of amplification of this mandate. The first, saw the role of the army change from peacekeeping to counterterrorism operations in Operation Pawan.[48] This was necessitated by the breakdown of peace talks with the Liberation Tigers of Tamil Eelam (LTTE) and conduct of operations against them thereafter. The second example relates to a change in the army's border guarding role against external threats. Until 1988 in J&K, the army was tasked to ensure the sanctity of the LoC. The commencement of proxy war by Pakistan thereafter required the adoption of a posture against both external threats and infiltration of terrorists. In addition to this, the army was also mandated to carry out CI operations in the hinterland during the initial years, until the RR was raised and became effective. These changes were driven by political directives as well as military threats and were part of a changing politico-military strategy. These were the result of a top-down approach and led to a major military change in the nature of responsibilities of the army.

NOTES

1. See *Field Service Regulations: Part I Operations, 1909*, His Majesty's Stationary Office, London, 1912, pp. 191-192, at http://ia700300.us.archive.org/17/items/pt1fieldservicer00greauoft/pt1fieldservicer00greauoft.pdf (Accessed September 3, 2013).
2. General Sir Andrew Skeen, "Preface", *Passing it On: Fighting the Pashtun on Afghanistan's Frontier*, Gale and Polden, Aldershot, 1932, A Republished and Annotated Edition, (eds.), United States Government, as represented by the Secretary of the Army, Foreign Military Studies Office, Fort Leavenworth, 2010, p. 3, at http://www.benning.army.mil/Library/content/Skeen%20-%20Passing%20It%20On%2030%20Nov%202010.pdf (Accessed September 4, 2013).
3. Ibid., p.114.
4. See Subir Bhaumik, *Insurgent Crossfire: Northeast India*, Lancers Publishers, New Delhi, 2008, p, 63.
5. The input was received from an officer who was in the Indian Military Academy in 1965 and confirmed reading the book as part of recommended reading during training.
6. See B.G. Verghese, *India's Northeast Resurgent: Ethnicity, Insurgency, Governance, Development*, Konark Publishers, New Delhi, 2002, pp. 16-19.
7. The British forces undertook a series of expeditions into the Naga areas commencing from 1866.
8. For the impact of political factors, see: Rajesh Rajagopalan, *Fighting Like a Guerrilla: The Indian Army and Counterinsurgency*, Routledge, New Delhi, 2008, pp. 143-149.
9. Sarvepalli Gopal, *Jawaharlal Nehru: A Biography, Vol 2, 1947-1956*, Oxford University Press, Delhi, 2010, p. 212.
10. Quoted in Rajesh Rajagopalan, No. 8, p. 147.
11. Lt Gen. Mathew Thomas in an interview to the author. Quoted in Lt Col. Vivek Chadha, *Low Intensity Conflicts in India: An Analysis*, Sage Publications, New Delhi, 2005, p. 342. The quote is in context with operations in Mizoram immediately after the induction of the Indian Army into the area.
12. Lt Col. S.P. Anand, "Counter Insurgency Theory and Practice in Mizo Hills", *USI Journal*, CI (423), 1971, p. 154.
13. For a detailed description of how conventional operations influenced the army in CI operations, see: Rajesh Rajagopalan, No. 8, pp. 156-158.
14. Vijendra Singh Jafa, "Insurgencies in North-East India: Dimensions of Discord and

Containment", in S.D. Muni (ed.), *Responding to Terrorism in South Asia*, Manohar Books, New Delhi, 2006, p. 96.

15. Lt Col. S.P. Anand, No. 12, p. 153.
16. Ibid., pp. 154-155.
17. Vijendra Singh Jafa, No. 14, p. 98.
18. Brig. S.K. Sinha, "Counter Insurgency Operations", *USI Journal*, C (420), July 1970, pp. 262-263.
19. Ibid., p. 263.
20. Ibid., p. 266.
21. Ibid., p. 268.
22. See "India: Military Court Fails Victims in Kashmir Killings", *Human Rights Watch*, January 24, 2014, at http://www.hrw.org/news/2014/01/24/india-military-court-fails-victims-kashmir-killings, (Accessed on April 29, 2014); "Amnesty Chides New Delhi", *Greater Kashmir*, December 13, 2012, at http://jammu.greaterkashmir.com/news/2012/Dec/13/amnesty-chides-new-delhi-39.asp (Accessed April 29, 2014).
23. See *Doctrine for Sub Conventional Operations (DSCO)*, Integrated Headquarters of Ministry of Defence (Army), Headquarters Army Training Command, Shimla, December 2006, p. 21.
24. Ibid., pp. i-ii.
25. Ibid., p. 20.
26. Ibid., p. 29.
27. Ibid., p. 30.
28. The army's decision to allow the police to develop its CI capabilities and present a civilian face was earlier witnessed during the Punjab terrorism period in the eighties and early nineties. Over a period of time, Punjab Police developed the necessary skills to handle the threat and take the lead in counterterrorism operations.
29. See *DSCO*, No. 23, p. 32.
30. Ibid., p. 35.
31. Ibid., "Foreword" (Gen J. J. Singh), p. i.
32. The Constitution of India, under Article 370, grants J&K, special status. In addition to this, on a number of occasions, successive prime ministers have called for "maximum autonomy" for the state. See "Restore Autonomy to Bring Peace in J&K: Ruling NC to Centre", *India Today*, June 17, 2012, at http://indiatoday.intoday.in/story/nc-autonomy-centre-jammu-and-kashmir/1/201100.html (Accessed November 20, 2013).
33. For the Air Chief's opinion on not employing "offensive airpower" for anti-Naxal operations given the possibility of "heavy collateral damage", see: "No Army Help for Anti-Naxal Operations: Chief General V.K. Singh", *The Times of India*, April 3, 2010, at http://articles.timesofindia.indiatimes.com/2010-04-03/india/28142881_1_anti-naxal-operations-internal-security-paramilitary-forces (Accessed November 12, 2013).
34. The assessment includes: The Naga insurgency in two stages – the first from 1954 to 1975 and the second from 1980 till 2014. The first was resolved, even as the second continues. The Mizo insurgency from 1966 to 1986, which was resolved. The insurgency in Manipur, from 1964 till date, which remains unresolved. The United Liberation Front of Assam (ULFA) from 1979, as an unresolved insurgency. The Bodo Liberation Tigers in Assam from 1996 till 2003 was successfully resolved. However the National Democratic Front of Bodoland (NDFB) from 1986 remains active till date. Punjab was a terrorist movement active from 1981 till 1994 and was successfully subdued. The Naxal insurgency commenced in 1967 and continues till date without successful resolution of the conflict. The J&K struggle

commenced in 1989 and continues till date. Finally, The Gorkhaland insurgency commenced in 1980 and was resolved by 1988.

35. For an accurate assessment of existing numbers in J&K, see: H. S. Panag, "The Drift in the Valley", *The Indian Express*, December 18, 2013, at http://archive.indianexpress.com/news/the-drift-in-the-valley/1208937/1 (Accessed March 31, 2014).
36. See "The Armed Forces (Special Powers) Act, 1958", at http://indianarmy.nic.in/Site/RTI/rti/MML/MML_VOLUME_3/CHAPTER__03/457.htm (Accessed October 31, 2013).
37. For a historical review of AFSPA, see Pushpita Das, "The History of Armed Forces Special Powers Act", *Armed Forces Special Powers Act: The Debate*, Institute of Defence Studies and Analyses, 2012, pp. 10-21, at http://idsa.in/monograph/ArmedForcesSpecialPowersActThe Debate (Accessed April 18, 2014).
38. *Naga People's Movement, of Human ... vs Union of India*, Supreme Court of India, November 27, 1997, at http://indiankanoon.org/doc/1072165/ (Accessed March 31, 2014).
39. Krishnadev Calamur, "India's Fence Sparks Little Debate", *Space Daily*, March 10, 2004, at http://www.spacedaily.com/news/nuclear-india-pakistan-04d.html (Accessed April 18, 2014).
40. Vijendra Singh Jafa, No. 14, p. 98.
41. The Salwa Judum, an experiment to employ tribal youth as local militia (Special Police Officers), was banned by the Supreme Court of India. See J. Venkatesan, "Salwa Judum Is Illegal, Says Supreme Court, *The Hindu*, July 5, 2011, at http://www.thehindu.com/news/national/salwa-judum-is-illegal-says-supreme-court/article2161246.ece (Accessed November 12, 2013).
42. See Praveen Swami, "Tackling Terror", *Frontline*, 5 (10), May 09-22, 1998, at http://www.frontline.in/static/html/fl1510/15100650.htm (Accessed April 09, 2014).
43. See Lt Col. Vivek Chadha, No. 11, p. 342.
44. Vivek Chadha, "India's Counterinsurgency Campaign in Mizoram", in Sumit Ganguly and David Fidler (eds.), *India and Counterinsurgency: Lessons Learned*, Routledge, New York, 2009, p. 37.
45. Vijendra Singh Jafa, "Insurgencies in North-East India: Dimensions of Discord and Containment", No. 14, p. 96.
46. Aloke Tikku, "Army Nixes Govt Plan to Hit Naxals from Air", *The Hindustan Times*, April 02, 2013, at http://www.hindustantimes.com/india-news/newdelhi/army-nixes-govt-plan-to-hit-naxals-from-air/article1-1036158.aspx (Accessed November 12, 2013).
47. See *DSCO*, No. 23, p. 3.
48. Ashok K. Mehta, "India's Counterinsurgency Campaign in Sri Lanka", in Sumit Ganguly and David Fidler (eds.), *India and Counterinsurgency: Lessons Learned*, Routledge, New York, 2009, pp. 163-164.

6

ORGANISATIONAL CHANGE

The Indian Army attempted structural changes with an aim of improving the efficiency of the organisation almost immediately after the experience of the first few years in counterinsurgency (CI) operations after independence. These changes were undertaken at both the strategic as well as tactical levels. While the former represented a deliberate and conscious decision which had an impact on a larger body of troops, the latter was more in the form of improvisations. However, irrespective of the level, these changes provide insight into the basis for undertaking these changes, and help suggest the reasons for their success or failure, as well as the advantages and limitations. While the chapter will limit its scope to the description of the case studies, these will be analysed further in greater detail, as part of the larger assessment of changes in CI operations in Chapter 8.

Creation of Ad Hoc Rifle Company

The infantry battalions are the biggest contributor to CI operations. They are instrumental in ensuring boots on ground, in order to effectively dominate the area and carry out precision strikes. However, this manpower intensive requirement was constrained during the initial years in CI operations. The battalions were organised for conventional operations, wherein four rifle companies formed the army's cutting edge. In addition, a support company carried heavy weapons like 3 inch mortars, and recoilless rifles. It was soon realised that this organisation, while suitable for conventional operations, was not the most efficient in terms of availability of manpower for a CI role. The terrain, nature of operations and need for accurate fire, which would cause least collateral damage, limited the use of heavy weapons. This led to local pooling of manpower within battalions with the dual aim of neutralising the organisational imbalance, and in the process, releasing additional manpower. This manpower was placed under an officer, by creating an ad hoc rifle company. Thus an infantry battalion which was designated to have four companies, now had five.[1] This method of limited military adjustment, in the face of operational threats, was a bottom-up example of military change. It addressed some of the existing limitations faced by battalions and facilitated better operational efficiency.[2]

The local improvisation carried out partially resolved existing organisational challenges at the battalion level. However, a number of limitations remained. Some of the critical ones were as follows:

- The changeover of an infantry battalion from an area after every two to three years, disrupted its intelligence network and neutralised the good work done there. A new battalion, which replaced it was forced to recommence these efforts, often from scratch.
- The primary role of infantry battalions was the defence of the country from external threats. This forced field formations and battalions to simultaneously retain focus on this role, even as they were involved in CI operations, thereby dividing their attention.
- The strength of infantry battalions got dissipated due to the allocation of almost a company worth of manpower for manning heavy fire support weapon systems. While this was important for conventional operations, these weapons had negligible utility in CI operations. This forced local level improvisations to recreate additional manpower. As mentioned earlier, an ad hoc company was created by reassigning these troops to meet the requirements of boots on the ground. While this proved to be effective in CI operations, it adversely impacted the training and battle worthiness of these troops.
- Infantry battalions are equipped keeping their conventional role in mind. Local procurement and sector specific weapons and stores

were purchased to make up additional critical requirements like battle vests and specialist vehicles. This made the set-up ad hoc and unreliable, as each case of procurement needed a long procedure to justify the need and was often prone to delays and contractual breakdowns. This affected the operational capability of these battalions.

Rashtriya Rifle Battalions

The Assam Rifles (AR), a paramilitary force, was raised in 1835 as the Cachar Levy. Officers from the army were inducted into the AR post-1884, and the association has continued since. This force was designated to provide security to areas in Northeast India. In order to address the limitation of a specialist force in Jammu and Kashmir (J&K), Rashtriya Rifle (RR) Battalions were raised. Though a previous experiment had been attempted in the form of 'I' Battalions for CI operations in Northeast India between 1968 and 1970, by re-designating a few infantry battalions, however, it was soon given up.[3] The RR was approved in 1990 and after a modest beginning, it expanded to a total of 63 battalions.[4] These battalions draw their men and officers from the Indian Army. The structure of the RR evolved over a period of time and attempted to overcome the limitations of infantry battalions in CI operations, as also provide the additional manpower critical for operations:

- RR battalions were affiliated to specific regiments of the army, thereby ensuring regimental linkages. Simultaneously, they also draw their troops from all arms and services to ensure a specialist cadre vis-à-vis infantry battalions.
- These battalions dispensed with heavy weapons to free additional manpower and have six, instead of four companies, thereby providing the much needed additional boots on the ground. Further, each RR battalion was authorised approximately 1,200 soldiers, as compared to 800 of an infantry battalion.
- RR battalions remain solely focussed on CI operations, thereby making them better suited for the role.
- The equipment profile of the battalions was tailored to ensure that every requirement peculiar to CI operations could be catered for within its resources.

- Even as soldiers were rotated over a period of two years, the battalions continue to remain in CI operations, thereby ensuring continuity and better adaptation to local needs and challenges.
- The raising of these battalions was accompanied by headquarters, which were tailored for CI operations and remained stationed permanently in the affected geographical areas. This helped them build an effective database of the area of operations, and in the process improved institutional memory.

Raising of RR battalions has been one amongst the few revolutionary changes, which have transformed the security dynamics of terrorism in J&K. This organisational change was also a much needed surge, which created continuity, expertise and effectiveness. It contributed to bringing down levels of violence and created a window of opportunity for any future political solution to the existing problem. The change was a top-down initiative, in the face of terrorist threats, and contributed towards a major transformation in the state's response to the ongoing proxy war.

Army Commander Special Financial Powers

The CI operations created conditions which required swift procurement of stores and equipment needed for the conduct of operations. However, delays as a result of existing long-drawn systems and procedures often led to poor operational preparedness. This was offset by delegating additional financial powers to army commanders, wherein they could sanction the procurement of equipment, thereby hastening existing procedures. This led to faster induction of stores and purchase of specialist equipment which had specific relevance for the area of operations. This change was a top-down attempt at improving efficiency, which ensured delegation of financial powers within the organisational structure of the army.

Commando Platoon

Yet another experiment within the infantry battalion led to manpower pooling to create an ad hoc sub-unit called the 'commando platoon'. This small group of soldiers was trained and equipped with the best available resources within the battalion and employed for special tasks assigned at both the formation and battalion levels.

The change of organisation of an infantry battalion in the early 1990s removed the need for local improvisation of commando platoons. Instead, a *Ghatak Platoon* was brought formally within the organisation of a battalion, thereby formalising the erstwhile arrangement. This platoon was suitably equipped, and has since been undertaking specialised operations. While the commando platoon was an example of limited bottom-up adjustment in order to meet operational threats, subsequent reorganisations followed up this initiative with a more formal arrangement.

NOTES

1. See Maj. R.D. Palsokar, "Fighting the Guerrilla", *USI Journal*, LXXXXI (385), Oct 1961, p. 270.
2. Since infantry battalions continue to be employed in a secondary role in CI operations, even as their primary role and organisation is suited for conventional operations, battalions carry out this local level improvisation in a bid to optimise manpower utilisation. The author, too, while commanding a battalion on the Line of Control (LoC) between India and Pakistan, in the J&K in 2007-08, resorted to this local adjustment to cover a larger area more effectively. He also witnessed its employment earlier during Operation Pawan against the Liberation Tigers of Tamil Eelam (LTTE) in Sri Lanka in 1989-1990.
3. See Rajesh Rajagopalan, *Fighting Like a Guerrilla: The Indian Army and Counterinsurgency*, Routledge, New Delhi, 2008, p. 162.
4. For a brief on the evolution of RR, see: B. Bhattacharya, "The Rashtriya Rifles", *Bharat Rakshak*, at http://www.bharat-rakshak.com/LAND-FORCES/Units/Infantry/222-Rashtriya-Rifles.html (Accessed November 20, 2013).

7

Change in Conduct of Operations

The operational focus of an army in counterinsurgency (CI) operations represents a critical aspect of its involvement. It not only represents the cutting edge of the force that is eventually employed, it is also the fulcrum that can tilt the balance of the eventual outcome in favour of the state. Unlike conventional wars where strategies and operational art are considered critical components of the war-waging potential of an army, operational issues remain paramount in CI operations. The concept of a strategic corporal came about as a result of the impact of the behaviour of even a single soldier, especially in the CI environment.[1] This is primarily related to the population of an area being considered as the centre of gravity of a struggle. This reinforces the need to place requisite emphasis on the relationship between the people and the forces that operate in an area.

There is a very large canvas that operational factors cover in CI operations. This not only includes the physical act of conducting operations, but also preparatory as well as post-operational issues like training and dealing with human rights accusations. This chapter will outline some of the changes that took place in this regard, as case studies, to better understand military change.

Changes in Conduct of Operations

The *Iron Fist with Velvet Glove* strategy was a manifestation of tactical changes that had evolved of a period of time. These changes reflected the operational imperatives of the army in CI operations, as also the need for people-friendly operations, transparency and accountability. It reinforced the need for battalions to acquire accurate intelligence through local sources and technical advancements.

Amongst the changes that took place was a reduction in the size of sub-units employed for operations. The initial years witnessed large-sized troop movements for operational manoeuvres. This was justified on the basis of heavy firepower requirement against terrorist groups, which could only be generated from a strength of 70 to 80 soldiers.[2] This numerical strength persisted, despite guerrillas deciding to move in smaller numbers to reduce their footprint along with the ability to merge with locals in the area. The decision to operate in larger groups was based on a number of factors. *First*, the conventional bias of the army continued to influence CI operations. This led to the view that companies and platoons were ideal fighting sub-units, despite a change in the operational context. *Second*, most operations were conducted with only generic intelligence. The absence of specific actionable intelligence limited the ability to carry out clinical strikes with small teams. *Third*, the reliance on a heavy volume of firepower to ensure operational superiority could only come from a larger number of weapons, which perforce required a bigger force.

This concept underwent a change when it was realised that a larger force was more cumbersome, inefficient and ineffective for CI operations. This was simultaneously accompanied by greater reliance on more specific and reliable intelligence, which enabled precision operations. The 2004 Indian Army Doctrine maintains this assertion:

> Resources of the security forces will invariably be spread over a large area of responsibility. In such an environment, operations based on small teams backed by good or specific intelligence increase the chance of contact with and success against the insurgents.[3]

This led battalions to become more nimble, flexible and adaptable to the inherently fluid nature of CI operations.

Yet another change experienced in the conduct of operations was a shift from large-scale cordon and search operations based on generic intelligence to clinical operations on the basis of specific intelligence. This relied on both human and technical intelligence. Over a period of time, army's intelligence teams managed a steady penetration in local areas. This was supplemented by sophisticated equipment for monitoring terrorist communications. As a result, the ensuing operations became swift, caused limited collateral damage and did not alienate the population. The initial forays into this highly specialised field began in the mid-nineties and over the years, in addition to the army, a number of intelligence and enforcement agencies, which function in close liaison with the army, developed similar sophisticated capabilities with success.[4]

Besides the military component of CI operations, equitable emphasis was also placed on the hearts and minds battle. This required special initiatives aimed at winning peace, after a degree of stability had been achieved. Based on the overall hearts and minds strategy of the army, commanders were given the liberty to fine tune it according to local conditions. Amongst the initiatives that gained considerable traction amongst the population was one called "heart as a weapon", which according to its proponent targeted the hearts of the population with the aim of weaning them away from terrorist propaganda. It aimed to subjugate the arrogance of power through the goodness of attitude.[5] The Corps Commander responsible for the initiative said: "The AK-47 is not my weapon. It's a mere tool to be used occasionally. The heart is my weapon."[6]

Training

The initial phase of CI operations witnessed the absence of pre-induction training. This was largely addressed by on-the-job training at the battalion level. While past experience in conventional operations ensured a degree of expertise in fundamental tactical skills used in patrolling, ambushes, raids, musketry and field craft, specific issues related to counterinsurgency had to be learnt on the job, in the absence of formal training facilities and mechanisms. This led to induction of troops into difficult operational conditions with inadequate understanding of CI operations. The regimental history of a Gurkha battalion highlights this very limitation. Referring to operations of an infantry battalion, it underlines that the battalion "had been inducted into this counter-insurgency area (Nagaland) without any specialised training."[7] Battalions deployed in the area adapted to the circumstances based on their experiences. A veteran of CI operations during the mid-sixties said: "But we learnt on the way, we learnt very quickly I would say."[8] On-the-job training remained the norm until May 1, 1970, when the first Counter Insurgency Jungle Warfare (CIJW) School was established at Veirangte, Mizoram. A similar situation came up when the army was deployed for CI operations in Sri Lanka, commencing from 1987. Troops were inducted without the requisite pre-induction training and perforce learnt the hard way through on-the-job training instead.[9] The initial induction for operations in Punjab, as well as Jammu and Kashmir (J&K), followed a similar trend. In J&K, pre-induction training was formalised with the establishment of Corps Battle Schools (CBS), wherein training became compulsory before induction into any CI area.

It is evident from the army's involvement in CI operations that training was planned and executed at two levels. The establishment of training schools like the premier institution at Veirangte was a major top-down change that has since served as the fulcrum of training activities for individuals and units deployed in Northeast India. Its establishment was necessitated by the nature of evolving threats and the need to better prepare soldiers for it.

On the other hand, every battalion of the army established its respective drills and procedures for on-the-job training, which remain flexible, and responded almost immediately to the nature of operations, induction of new equipment and techniques to improve effectiveness. While this can be considered a limited change, its impact is no less than structured training offered by large institutions like the one at Veirangte. Under circumstances like those prevalent in Sri Lanka, it played a very important role. The battalions which were inducted for operations did not receive any formal pre-induction training. In fact, most units had been involved in training for conventional operations of a completely different kind, including some which had their operational role in deserts. Their sudden induction into an unfamiliar CI environment left the battalion commanders with little option other than adjusting to the fast-changing conditions and disseminating these through on-the-job unit level training. In most cases, unit commanders retained decentralised control over this form of training, with the option of further delegating it to sub-unit commanders. Training on improvised explosive devices (IEDs), newly inducted AK-47 rifles and its clones from other East European countries, radio sets, secrecy equipment, rocket launchers and Liberation Tigers of Tamil Eelam (LTTE) tactics was conducted frequently to keep troops updated.[10]

Readjustment of Battalions

Unlike a major surge in force levels, localised readjustment of forces is a more common method of improving operational efficiency. This is done as a result of changing threat perceptions, which may emerge due to shifting concentration of terrorists in a given area, thereby making the CI grid dynamic in nature. This limited military change is an example of both bottom-up approach and top-down assessment based on comparative inputs received from different sources of information. However, irrespective of the method of initiation of the process, it does not bring about major changes in operational methodology, and its impact often remains localised.

Strengthening and Buffering Vehicles

The Indian Army faced its first major brush with IEDs and large-scale use of mines in CI operations against the LTTE in Sri Lanka. This led to changes in drills and procedures for patrols to ensure that casualties could be minimised. However, unlike foot patrols, where gaps between soldiers, careful examination of ground conditions and avoidance of beaten tracks helped reduce casualties, it was more difficult for protecting groups of soldiers in vehicles. Transport-bound soldiers provided viable and high visibility targets for the LTTE. As a result, a large number of units improvised at the battalion level, with support from brigade workshops to reinforce and strengthen vehicles. Additional metal sheets and wooden planks to reinforce side panels, and sandbags on the vehicle floor were some of the limited military adjustments carried out. This reaction to operational threats was a bottom-up example of adaptation, and while not perfect, it did provide a degree of additional protection. It also enhanced the confidence of soldiers, who felt better protected in case of an eventuality.

The challenge of IEDs and mines was only partially overcome by limited military modification of vehicles. A more comprehensive solution was the procurement and deployment of Casspir mine protected vehicles (MPVs).

Use of Captured Equipment

The initial phase of operations in Sri Lanka by the Indian Army brought to the fore the relative disadvantage vis-à-vis the LTTE, in terms of basic tactical weapons and equipment,[11] including radio sets used. As compared to the inefficient and laborious ANPRC-25 sets of the army, which were not secure and had a limited range, the LTTE used Motorola, Yaesu and Kenwood sets. These worked on a different frequency band, had longer range and were far lighter and more reliable. Over a period of time, battalions captured a number of these radio sets. The captured sets thereafter became force multipliers for monitoring LTTE communication.

In a similar way, the army was at a disadvantage against terrorists in J&K. While the terrorists were using the AK series of rifles, the army continued to be equipped with the 7.62 mm self-loading rifles (SLRs). During the initial years, a large number of terrorist rifles and radio sets were captured. Given the obvious disadvantage faced by soldiers, each battalion was issued with a limited number of captured rifles and radio sets. This enhanced their fundamental capability, and simultaneously gave them the ability to monitor communication on these captured sets, at least during the initial years. These were examples of bottom-up limited military change, which enabled the conduct of electronic warfare in CI operations and helped equip soldiers better. It also reduced casualties and gave operational parity with terrorists.

Modification of SLR

As in the case of radio sets, the LTTE was at an advantage with respect to the personal weapon of soldiers. The infantry battalions carried the standard issue SLR. This fired single shot rounds and was plagued by repeated stoppages. On the other hand, the LTTE was armed with the AK-47 rifle, which was undoubted better suited for CI operations and was widely considered as the most reliable weapon for guerrilla warfare. An attempt was made by local workshops in the army to give a multiple round fire capability to the SLR. However, this modification was not successful, and finally led to the induction of East European clones of the AK-47 rifles during the second half of army's deployment in 1989. The initial change was an attempt at limited military adjustment, as part of a bottom-up approach, as a result of the operational threat faced by the army. Subsequent inductions were top-down instead and went a long way in making solders better equipped to face the challenge at hand.

Technology-driven Changes

Technology has remained a major driver of change in the conduct of warfare. However, unlike conventional threats, CI operations are not affected as much by technological changes, as a result of the nature of warfare and adversary.[12] Despite this reality, given the advantage of resources at the disposal of the state, it would be easy to presume that the insurgents are at a distinct disadvantage, when compared to the army. However, in case of the Indian Army, this was not always the case. The LTTE was better equipped in terms of their personal weapons and communication equipment. Similarly, the early years in J&K also witnessed a similar reality. Some of the examples cited above highlight the technological disadvantage faced by battalions. Similarly, even where adaptation was carried out, it was a mix of proactive and reactive measures in the face of adversity.

Night-vision and Surveillance Devices

The use of night-vision devices in conventional conflicts has been a reality for long. It forced a change in how night operations were planned and fought. However, this change did not come about in a similar fashion in case of CI operations. While the army made good use of night-vision devices, as part of its progressive modernisation, insurgent groups and terrorists did not have access to it in the Indian environment. This provided a distinct edge to the army and reversed the advantage terrorists enjoyed in case of night operations, given their ability to better exploit local terrain under most circumstances. The induction of night-vision devices was not only seen as part of crew-served weapons like medium machine guns, but also hand-held thermal imagers and night sights for personal rifles, sniper rifles and light machine guns.

Surveillance devices also gave a similar advantage. It enabled the army in conjunction with other supporting forces to better monitor and in a number of cases locate terrorists. Operations on the Line of Control (LoC) especially received a boost as a result of these inductions. Surveillance centres were now able to track and monitor terrorists approaching the fence. This enabled clinical operations timed to perfection in a bid to neutralise maximum terrorists. These changes limited the adverse impact of difficult terrain, weather and Pakistani interference to support infiltration. The induction was a top-down change, as a result of evolving threats, facilitated by improving technology, and brought about a major shift in operations.

Creation and Deployment of Ashi Pillai

Operations in CI operations require large-scale vehicular movement, both for operations and administrative support. However, there was a constant threat of remotely controlled IEDs, which had caused a number of casualties over the years. An officer from the Electronics and Mechanical Engineers (EME) was instrumental in locally adapting to the challenge and creating a device called Ashi Pillai, which could jam the remote signals of an IED, thereby neutralising the threat.[13] Vehicles were equipped with this device and became an integral part of military convoys thereafter, possibly saving innumerable lives. This bottom-up case of improvisation was subsequently adopted institutionally to make IED jammers an integral part of large convoys.

NOTES

1. Rye Barcott, "The Strategic Corporal", *Harvard Business Review*, October 21, 2010, at https://hbr.org/2010/10/the-strategic-corporal.html, accessed on Match 14, 2016.
2. Maj. R.V. Jatar, "Counter Insurgency Operations", *USI Journal*, LXXXXVIII (413), October 1968, p. 415.
3. *Indian Army Doctrine*, Army Training Command, Shimla, October 22, 2004, at ids.nic.in/Indian%20Army%20Doctrine/indianarmydoctrine_1.doc (Accessed July 1, 2015).
4. Pravin Swami documented this capability in 2000. Since then, there has been a marked improvement in this capability. See Pravin Swami, "Eyes and Ears Wide Open", *Frontline*, 17(9), April 29-May 12, 2000, at http://www.frontline.in/static/html/fl1709/17090230.htm (Accessed November 12, 2013).
5. Lt Gen. Syed Ata Hasnain, "The Heart Is My Weapon: Kashmir Revisited", *The War College Journal*, September 2011, 40 (1), p. 2.
6. "Interview: General Officer Commanding, 15 Corps, Lt Gen. Syed Ata Hasnain", *Force*, May 2011, at http://www.forceindia.net/Interviewmay2.aspx (Accessed November 4, 2011).
7. Brig. H. S. Sodhi and Brig. Prem K. Gupta, *History of 4th Gurkha Rifles (Vol IV), 1947-1971*, Delhi, 1985, p. 150.
8. Lt Gen. Mathew Thomas in an interview to the author. Quoted in Lt Col. Vivek Chadha, *Low Intensity Conflicts in India: An Analysis*, Sage Publications, New Delhi 2005, p. 342.
9. Ashok K. Mehta, "India's Counterinsurgency Campaign in Sri Lanka", in Sumit Ganguly and David Fidler (eds.), *India and Counterinsurgency: Lessons Learned*, Routledge, New York, 2009, p. 170.
10. Based on the author's experience in Operation Pawan in Sri Lanka.
11. Ashok K. Mehta, No. 9, p. 170.
12. CI operations have witnessed the use of night-vision devices, surveillance and monitoring equipment, which has served as a force multiplier in operations. However, in comparison with the conventional battlefield, the employment and exploitation have been relatively limited.
13. See "Corps of Electrical & Mechanical Engineers", GlobalSecurity.org, at http://www.globalsecurity.org/military/world/india/eme.htm (Accessed April 29, 2014).

8

Army's Ability to Cope with Change

Chapter 7 gives an overview of some of the challenges faced by the army, while dealing with CI operations. It also highlights the manner in which the Indian Army adapted and changed in order to improve its response over the years. The analysis is based on 27 cases of change in the Indian Army, as related to CI operations. In this chapter, each case of change has further been analysed based on the following parameters:

- **Type of Change.** An analysis of the case studies indicates that military change in CI operations can be classified as strategic, organisational or operational. Strategic changes impacted a very large cross section of the army. In most cases it also forced a major shift in the manner in which the army went about fulfilling its mandate. Organisational change, led to either limited or major shifts in the structure of the deployed forces. Finally, operational changes were limited and functional in nature and improved the conduct of tactical operations in field.
- **Approach to Change.** The approach to change has been assessed based on its initiation, which has been seen as either top-down or bottom-up. Its relevance is evident in strategic, organisational and operational changes.
- **Manifestation of Change.** The manifestation of change illustrates its scale and magnitude and can be classified as either major or limited. The parameters for this include the scale of change, number

of agencies involved, nature of change it resulted in and the impact it had as a result of the change. This could be in the form of limited changes, with a localised impact on how the organisation functions or behaves, or a major military shift, thereby substantially impacting the functioning of the army in CI operations.

- **Driver.** Operational threats emerged as the primary driver of military change. The other factors include technology, political directives, environmental pressures or a combination of these. As the subsequent analysis suggests, some of these can also function as shapers instead.
- **Impact.** The impact of military change is difficult to measure. However, the benefit of hindsight does provide the opportunity to assess it, and thereby its effectiveness. It is also important to analyse the timeliness and speed of change initiated, as also its quality.

Type of Change

Strategic changes were mostly military in nature, however, in a number of cases the influence and involvement of a political directive is evident. This is in keeping with the nature of CI or counterterrorism (CT) conflicts, which are essentially political in nature and more often than not, employ a military instrumentality to recapture the democratic space that is occupied by the terrorists.

An assessment of strategic changes clearly indicates that in most cases, these formed a part of an evolutionary process, rather than being revolutionary. The conduct of CI operations during different periods of post-independence history highlight stages of this learning process. The initial impact of conventional operations on CI operations was replaced by the influence of British experiences in Malaya. This commenced a shift from the search and clear strategy to clear and hold. However, this was further refined with experience, as the case study suggests. Cumulative learning led to adoption of improved strategies over a period of time and this culminated in the Iron Fist with Velvet Glove strategy. Amongst the exceptions to this evolutionary process are decisions to raise Rashtriya Rifles (RR) and establishment of the artificial obstacle system, which can be considered as revolutionary shifts. These transformed CT operations and successfully blunted the advantage enjoyed by the adversary.

While the decision to raise RR was a revolutionary decision, however, its follow-up systemic improvements have been an incremental process. During the initial years of deployment of RR, it became evident that even as its structure was suitable, its intake pattern needed a number of changes, in an attempt to fine-tune the limitations observed. This included closer affiliation with regiments of the infantry, armoured corps and artillery to ensure greater cohesion. These evolutionary changes led to an improvement in performance levels over a period of time, reinforcing the importance of this process.

At the tactical level, organisational changes were witnessed in the form of limited adjustments, in order to overcome some of the limitations imposed by existing structures. In the case of the infantry battalion, this was a result of the organisation tailored for conventional threats. The ad hoc creation of the commando platoon was more a need-based change, which was felt not only in CI but also in conventional operations. This eventually led to the creation of a Ghatak Platoon in the new organisation of an infantry battalion.

Operational changes, as the case studies suggest, despite being significant, represented the tactical battlefield in CI operations. These changes were spearheaded by leaders, who were willing and capable of adapting to emerging and existing challenges. Even as operational changes seem relatively insignificant, especially in relation to strategic and organisational changes, however, in CI operations, their significance cannot be underestimated. Seemingly insignificant changes are capable of making an appreciable impact on the conduct of operations and result in reduction of casualties. The ability to monitor communications of terrorist networks, neutralising improvised explosive devices (IEDs) along important arteries are some of these examples. Since operations are conducted primarily at the battalion level, limited military changes within a battalion can improve its effectiveness substantially.

All three types of change (i.e. strategic, organisational or operational) represent different levels of decision-making. If levels are visualised on an ascending scale, then operational changes are likely to find place at the lowest, organisational changes at the lowest or highest level and finally strategic changes primarily at the highest level. Since strategic and organisational changes initiated at higher levels represent major shifts, their initiation and implementation is likely to face greater resistance.[1] This is not merely a result of inter-agency conflicts of interest and financial outlays, but challenges in successful implementation, given the large-scale changes envisaged. (This specific aspect will be dealt with as part of the discussion on impact, later in the book.) As the level of initiation and implementation is lowered, change is easier to achieve. Its impact is also easily perceptible, which allows more flexibility to achieve desired objectives. As an illustration, it is easier to change the modifications of a locally adapted vehicle for the protection of troops, rather than changing the general services qualitative requirement (GSQR) as part of the formal acquisition process.

Changes are not rigid or necessarily permanent in nature. Since changes are driven by circumstances and conditions in the form of drivers, the possibility of some of these changes being reversed or modified cannot be ruled out. As an example, the additional forces inducted as a result of the Kargil conflict, were retained in Jammu and Kashmir (J&K) immediately after the culmination of the conflict. Some of these forces were employed for CT operations to assist in stabilising the CI grid. However, most troops were subsequently withdrawn, after they helped lower violence levels substantially. This made the process of surge reversible. Similarly, an infantry battalion carries out limited organisational change locally only for the duration of its stay in CI operations. These changes are reversed immediately on de-induction from the area of operations.

The army evolved over a period of time to carry out precision and clinical operations, which became the cornerstone of the Iron Fist with Velvet Glove strategy. However, this was made possible by a well-established intelligence network, which in turn was a result of diligent efforts by the army over a long period of time. In case the army is inducted into a new area of operations, a reasonable period of time would be required to establish a similar network and the ability to implement all facets of the strategy. This could become a difficult proposition in the initial phase. Therefore, even as the broad parameters of the strategy remain in place, however, its building blocks would need adjustment in the initial phase of operations. This could also be impacted by a relatively higher degree of opposition, which would need a greater proportion of kinetic operations to establish a semblance of order and stability before population support measures can be rolled out in their entirety.[2]

Approach to Change and Its Manifestation

The approach to change, as seen from the case studies, has been either top-down or bottom-up. The top-down approach has usually been initiated from the highest levels in the army, or at times even at the political level. While the broad direction of CI operations emanated from Prime Minister Jawaharlal Nehru, it continues to be guided by subsequent leaders at the central and state level. Even though the army is not deployed in operations against left-wing extremism (LWE), however, quite clearly, the guidelines for its implementation have been provided by Prime Minister Manmohan Singh and home ministers over a period of time.[3] The military strategy based on political directions has emanated time and again from the office of the Chief of the Army Staff, as is evident from the army's Doctrine for Sub Conventional Operations (DSCO). However, its implementation is often delegated at the command and corps level, from where detailed instructions as relevant to specific areas emanate.

At the other end of the spectrum, considerable changes have also been bottom-up. These were experimented with and implemented locally to adjust to circumstances. Over a period of time, based on their effectiveness, these changes were introduced formally. Examples like using captured radio sets for monitoring communication in Sri Lanka and undertaking small team precision operations began at the tactical level. Subsequently, electronic warfare received attention at the highest level and was formalised as part of the overall CI strategy. Similarly, small team precision operations find mention in the DSCO, well after its introduction at the tactical level.

Despite a seemingly clear distinction between the two approaches to change, there is an underlying linkage between the two. Various bottom-up changes, which were implemented successfully, became the basis for the initiation of a strategy or doctrine, with smaller changes serving as its building blocks. The Iron Fist with Velvet Glove strategy, could not have been articulated and implemented, without the efficacy of its elements having been tested in operations with a degree of success. In other cases, the formulation of a strategy was followed up by its implementation in areas and amongst formations, which may not have done so, given the resistance to change. There is thus, a complementarity in the approach to change, even as its formal initiation begins in one of these ways.

In addition to the initiation process of military change, which may, for example, begin as bottom-up, only to finally get implemented as a larger top-down shift, its subsequent success eventually hinges upon successful implementation at the functional level. This challenge is especially critical in case of top-down initiation of change, wherein its mere initiation is not a guarantee for eventual success. Successful change is ultimately a result of its adoption at the grass-roots level, which in turn creates a major shift that the change envisages. This further reinforces the close linkage between limited and major military changes and finally its implementation, which may yet again involve adjustments at the tactical level.

The approach to change is closely linked with its manifestation. While it is not a rule, however, it is only in exceptional circumstances that the top-down changes have been a result of limited military adjustment, and bottom-up changes have resulted in major shifts. More often than not, major changes have been top-down, while limited military adjustments are bottom-up. There are exceptions like the amendment in Armed Forces (Special) Powers Act [AFSPA], which was a top-down process, however, it can only be classified as a limited military change. Similarly, the designation of some battalions as "I" battalions was top-down; however, it was a limited change, which was eventually discarded. As has been highlighted earlier, the roots of a major change could well link it with earlier limited changes undertaken at the tactical level by junior leaders.

Drivers of Change

The drivers of military change emerge as its most important linkage. In order to analyse the role of drivers, it is important to understand a driver's meaning and implication in relation to military change. Drivers function as triggers and catalysts for change, in the case of both limited as well as major shifts. If this is seen in the context of a variable in the form of operational challenges and a constant like the army as an organisation in CI operations, then the role of a driver is very similar to its context in modern-day information technology (IT) equipment. IT is driven by two components. While the hardware is a constant like the army, the software, is a variable, much like operational challenges, given its constant state of evolution. If the software has to connect to the hardware, a set of drivers are required to ensure that both can talk to each other and the capability of the hardware can best be exploited. Drivers in terms of military change also perform a similar function. They provide the trigger, connect and necessary push for the military to adapt to operational conditions.

The most common driver that emerges in the case studies analysed is operational threat. The emergence and evolution of threats force militaries to not only fine tune their own strategy in a CI area but also provide the impetus to explore means to remain a step ahead of terrorists. This is a challenging requirement, as in more cases than not, given the inherent flexibility of terrorist groups, their networks, as well as their better survival instincts, they tend to remain ahead of the innovation curve. This implies that militaries are likely to play catch-up and will remain reactive in their approach, despite best efforts to the contrary.

This limitation is likely to affect military effectiveness, unless change, at all stages of its evolution, is implemented with foresight and the ability to exploit inherent strengths of the army, even as its weaknesses are effectively managed. Most changes at the tactical level, which entail limited adjustments best adapt to localised terrorist innovations. They are often the first to notice these, as also the most affected by it. The use of open radio communications by terrorists was neutralised by the ability to monitor it. Similarly, the employment of codes rather than open messages thereafter was beaten by breaking these over a period of time. The switch to cell phones was challenged by effective monitoring capability. All these were examples of limited changes carried out in reasonably good time, though it remained reactive as the examples suggest.

On the other hand, an initiative aimed at making operations more people friendly through precision strikes rather than cordon and search and implementing stricter rules of engagement, which ensure minimal collateral damage, transparency and accountability, creates a long-term advantage over terrorists. Even if these are undertaken as a reaction to criticism to begin with, it can subsequently not only negate the limitations imposed by reactive policies, in the long run, but can also regain traction amongst the population at large.

Technology is considered an important driver for military change. However, unlike conventional operations, the case studies indicate that it has not played as critical a role as operational threats. Even where technology is seen as a trigger, it is so in conjunction with operational threats, which provide the reason for technology to be exploited for a given purpose. The Line of Control (LoC) obstacle system came up as a result of operational threats. It was, however, reinforced and made more effective by the use of technology, which was tailored to the fence. Similarly, the Ashi Pillai equipment was an example of adapting existing technology for a threat which required adjusting to changed terrorist tactics for long. Therefore, these cases were examples of technology functioning more as a shaper, rather than a driver. However, the success of precision intelligence-based operations, was driven by technology. It enabled a shift from cordoning large areas and increasing the possibility of collateral damage to targeting specific operations. This reduced public anger against frequent operations in populated areas, and thereby reduced alienation. It also helped build intelligence as a result of this change.

Political directions rarely end up initiating military change. This is essentially because most changes are a result of operational threats and availability of technology, and political decision-making has a limited impact on them. However, one area, which deeply influences military change is the change in army's goals or objectives. This can potentially result in a change in military strategy in order to achieve them. The most striking example of changing goals was witnessed during the Indian Peace Keeping Force (IPKF) deployment in Sri Lanka, as part of Op Pawan.[4] The role of the Indian Army changed from peacekeeping to CI after breakdown of talks with the Liberation Tigers of Tamil Eelam (LTTE). An army, which had been inducted into the area to disarm the LTTE peacefully, was directed to undertake some of the bloodiest CI campaigns undertaken in its history. This change in threat perception, forced a change in military strategy. The lack of preparation, intelligence and support required for such an operation forced both major military shifts, as also limited but fast adaptation by battalions, which had little choice but to undertake on-the-job training.

Environmental pressure, while usually not a driver, does emerge as an important shaper of change. The environment in a CI area, which could include pressure from the people, media or even local political leaders, can create conditions which can facilitate change. However, there can also be specific cases, which are driven by environmental pressure, in which case, this does become a driver of change. The amendment of AFSPA was driven by environmental pressure, as a result of which select representatives of the people filed a case in the Supreme Court. On the contrary, the decision to avoid cordon and search operations was driven by operational considerations, but shaped by environmental pressures. In contrast to political directives, which emerge as a driver, the prevailing political environment can be a shaper for military change.

Impact of Military Change

The examples cited above illustrate almost without exception that military change in CI operations improved the effectiveness of the army. The example of protected villages and modification to existing SLR rifles being some of the exceptions. This leads to the obvious conclusion that change enhances effectiveness. Empirical evidence seems to support this conclusion. However, it deserves a more detailed assessment based on its quality, pace and resultant impact, in order to understand the challenges.

Source of Influence

The first aspect which merits assessment is whether change in the army came about as a result of internal mechanisms, or whether it was more a case of external circumstances and pressures.

At the strategic level, the army's shift from expeditionary operations before independence to treating insurgents as misguided youth thereafter came about as a result of both political direction as well as guidance from the highest levels within the army. In contrast, subsequent strategic changes were undertaken primarily by the army, based on its assessment of threats and evolutionary adaptation over a period of time. The lessons learnt by the army during the initial years in CI operations led to the evolution of its approach. This was further refined according to the nature of local challenges faced. The 2006 doctrine for sub-conventional operations is an example of this internal churning within the army. At the organisational and operational levels, changes were a result of the army's internal assessment of its requirements, as well as limited local adaptation in the face of adversity.

In addition to the external impact from the political decision-making authority, environmental views and pressures also shaped military change. The Iron Fist with Velvet Glove doctrine, besides being a product of the army's long years of experience, was also influenced by the increasing pressure from the people at large, media and human rights groups to minimise collateral damage and civilian casualties. This pressure forced greater accountability and transparency in the functioning of the army in CI operations.[5]

The evolution of the army's approach to CI operations has also been a product of cross-pollination of transnational experiences of other armies, though primarily during the preliminary phases. The initial attempt at formulating a strategy for CI operations was influenced by ideas implemented earlier in campaigns like Malaya, as is evident from the adoption of Briggs Plan and the creation of model villages in both Nagaland and Mizoram. Similarly, operations in Kenya possibly led to the use of pseudo gangs. The use of borrowed ideas in CI operations eventually lost impact after some of these experiments failed to deliver desirable results.

The changes were therefore both adaptive and emulative, more often than not following an evolutionary path. There are few cases where these have proved to be revolutionary, as seen from the case studies.

Quality of Change

The quality of change is an important aspect of change management. The army has successfully overcome the challenge of raising new organisations, as seen from the example of RR battalions. It also established an effective obstacle system in the form of the LoC fence, substantially cutting down infiltration from Pakistan. The evolution of the DSCO, and its successful implementation is yet another example of successfully adapting to change. At the operational level, a number of limited changes at the local level successfully blunted the advantage and initiative of insurgents repeatedly.

While these are the positives of change management, it is equally pertinent to look into the effectiveness of some organisations created and tasked to deal with challenges like information warfare, cyberwarfare and perception management. The setting up of specialist organisations can only be effective, when officers and men with the requisite training and experience are posted there. The existing manpower policies have not been able to manage this requirement, with other conflicting conditions like maintaining regional posting profiles and inadequate profiling of officers on areas of expertise. This leads to a steep learning curve and inadequate contribution for highly specialised responsibilities. It has also led to establishment of organisations with a suitable mandate, but with inadequate capability inputs to achieve it.[6]

This limitation is also affected by the lack of specialist culture in the Indian Army. There are no cyber specialists or information warfare specialists, who continue to work in their area of specialisation, beyond their limited, mandated tenures. The army continues to be led by what is often referred to as generalists or general duty (GD) officers. Even where these officers are able to develop a degree of specialisation, the pressure to hold the next criteria appointment often takes precedence over retaining domain knowledge.

The inability to create a pool of specialists is also affected by the inability to acknowledge, nurture and encourage intellectual pursuits. This links closely with the absence of specialists. Officers who display such ability do not have the option to pursue specialisation, since it clashes with the existing system of officer management in the army. While the impact of this limitation is marginal at the battalion level, it magnifies thereafter, given the need for greater awareness and understanding, which is enabled by intellectual inputs, in order to facilitate informed decision-making.[7] The lack of these inputs is detrimental to the initiation and pursuit of change management.

Quality of change demands continuity of ideas and their implementation. The short tenures of senior commanders in the army, often limited to just one year in chair as a corps commander, severely impact the ability to ensure successful incubation, nurturing and implementation of military change. Continuity in appointments is constrained by a linear progress of careers in the army, wherein an officer is required to hold the appointment of a corps commander in order to become an army commander, and thereafter the Chief of the Army Staff. This is unlike the US Army, wherein a capable officer like David Petraeus was moved from the US Central Command to Force Commander International Security Assistance Force (ISAF) in Afghanistan, which in the Indian context could well be seen as a demotion, purely from a hierarchical perspective. These factors have had a negative influence on the ability of the army to bring about quality changes at the strategic level in a suitable time frame.

At the operational level, the army has often inducted into different areas of operations with minimal preparation and warning. The initial induction of the army in Sri Lanka was with a backpack, as a peacekeeping force. However, as events there and elsewhere proved, the battalions had little option but to react to circumstances and adapt to them at the grass-roots level. This has consistently been one of the intrinsic strengths of the army, and in many ways the reason for it handling every challenge with a degree of success. Operational changes were not only a result of limited yet important adjustments, they also influenced the evolution of most major shifts that took place at the strategic level. Even organisational changes began as ad hoc measures well before they were formally implemented. These include commando platoons as Ghatak platoons, ad hoc companies as a prelude to its formalisation as additional companies in RR, strengthening of vehicles and employing captured equipment – the list can be endless with regards to tactical adaptation by the army. Since junior leadership is the most critical facet of CI operations, its ability to adapt at the tactical level has made up repeatedly for systemic deficiencies.[8]

Speed of Implementation

The speed of implementing military change is important to ensure that an organisation remains prepared for future challenges. Change management merely as a reaction to emerging threats and challenges keeps an army behind the curve of fast-moving events. There have been few cases, wherein the army has been able to pre-empt situations by adapting to future challenges. For example, in almost every case, as highlighted in the previous section, training institutions were set up well after the induction of troops in the areas of CI operations. The army was inducted into Nagaland in 1955; however, the Counter Insurgency and Jungle Warfare (CIJW) School came up only in 1970.[9] This led to avoidable casualties and loss of precious time in bringing troops up to requisite professional standards. The inadequacy of weapons and equipment was a serious challenge for soldiers deployed in Operation Pawan.[10] Despite this setback in 1987, the army was found wanting in its equipment profile during the initial years in J&K, which led to the use of captured weapons and equipment. Even as late as the Kargil Conflict, the army's equipment profile was well below par. General V.P. Malik, the Chief of the Army Staff during the conflict, made the famous statement on June 23, 1999,

"We shall fight with whatever we have."[11] He reinforces the limitations imposed by procedural red tape and writes:

> Keeping in view our shortages and deficiencies, we do not get adequate budgetary allocation. But even when we do get something, our procurement procedures are such that we can seldom spend the given amount.[12]

He adds a footnote:

> Besides lack of funds, our procedures are unresponsive, cost escalatory, frustrating and demoralising. Vendors create and exploit the 'scam phobia'. We do believe in self-reliance but the problem is that even in critical areas, the development and production agencies make promises, then fail to keep them for years on end.[13]

Therefore, changes were often brought about after reverses or events forced them upon the army, rather than due to a well-established system that foresaw and prepared for eventualities.

Constraints of Military Change

Over a period of time, the army has operated in a number of CI areas. It has changed, learnt lessons and improved its capacity to be more effective. However, change management is influenced by institutional memory and ready availability of declassified material.[14] Despite the winds of change having a major social impact on the army, certain policies in this regard have not changed. The declassification policy of documents – its accessibility to scholars – remains buried in bureaucratic hurdles. The failure to institutionalise the process of declassification thus remains one of the most important roadblocks to institutionalised learning of lessons from CI operations. The army has also failed to freely circulate assessments of past experiences in CI operations amongst successive generations of leaders. This lack of critical assessment of past successes and failures could result in leaders relearning past lessons, and worse, repeating past mistakes. It is important that lessons learnt be made freely available to units being inducted into CI areas and others, which are not classified to the public at large, to enable a broad-based debate on issues of critical importance.

One of the most consistent challenges faced by the army prior to its induction into a CI area has been the lack of adequate intelligence. In the past, intelligence was not only limited in relation to the conduct of operations, but also about terrorist groups it was required to deal with. More often than not, this led to the initial months being spent on attempts to find the right direction to operations. While at times it was related to the breakdown of governance structures in states, at others, it was a reflection of poor integration of different organisations as a cohesive inter-agency effort. It was also a reflection of limited capability of intelligence gathering, its collation and dissemination. Every operation reflected this limitation, especially during the initial period.

The success of CI operations is characterised by a well-functioning intelligence set-up. While it is not possible for the army to establish it in potential area of operations, intelligence agencies must be required to fill gaps and be held accountable for their inability to do so. The deployment of the army in Operation Bajrang is one such example. Over the first few months of the army's deployment, a list of leaders of the United Liberation Front of Assam (ULFA) had been drawn up. However, in some cases, the lack of intelligence was such that a local insurgent leader came to an army post, made an innocuous inquiry and left without the post being able to identify him. This was confirmed when the same leader called up to rub salt into the army's wounds![15] The conditions were not different in J&K, wherein 8 Mountain Division was inducted into the area, not only without preparation but also with limited intelligence concerning its area of operations. This led the battalions to focus a large part of their energy to this task. Under conditions, wherein the civil administration had virtually capitulated during this period and could not support the army, there were few options other than the inefficient cordon and search operations to collect intelligence.[16] This did more to alienate the people, than support the long-term aims of the army.

The army faced similar challenges during Operation Pawan. The limitations of inadequate intelligence as well as poor coordination between intelligence agencies in this case reinforces the aforementioned argument. Dr Kalyanaraman highlights some of these limitations as, the absence of intelligence assets in Sri Lanka, inadequate area specialisation of military intelligence officers, limited resources and capability of military intelligence and lack of training on handling prisoners and gathering intelligence from them.[17] This inadequacy was made worse by limited sharing of intelligence and lack of jointness between agencies. The local sensitivities in Tamil Nadu further exaggerated this challenge.[18]

Intelligence is one of the important pre-requisites for military change. It enables both faster and more informed decision-making. The absence of intelligence severely limits the ability to adapt to change, since it keeps the army in a reactionary state against terrorists and also places constraints on precision operations.

The success of a doctrine is based on its strategic and tactical implementation. While it is relatively easier to lay down strategic guidelines, tactical amplification of the same can prove to be a challenge. The army's shift to a more humane approach to operations was formalised with the enunciation of the DSCO. This was subsequently reinforced through measures at the Corps level, with the example of Heart as a Weapon initiative. The success of these guidelines, as has been highlighted earlier, hinges on their successful implementation. The reduction in human rights violations, collateral damage and alienation reinforces this to an extent. This was supported by stringent rules of engagement, strict operational procedures and guidelines. However, past experience in this context suggests that unless stringent measures are undertaken, there is a possibility of dissonance between the strategic and tactical understanding of directives. The fact that a former Chief of the Army Staff had to ban the use of the word "kills" emphasises the challenge faced by the army to implement operational guidelines.[19] These contradictions were partly a result of the inability to rationalise doctrines with human resources policies, wherein promotions and unit citations were influenced by "numbers", which inadvertently gave a fillip to notching up the highest number of "kills".

Applicability of Military Change to Specific Regions

The complexity of CI operations in India is affected by the diversity of threats posed by each separate region. Changes to emerging challenges came about at different stages of the army's employment in CI operations. A brief assessment of this evolutionary trend illustrates this timeline (**see Annexure 2**). It also highlights that the army was at its adaptive best at the tactical level in areas where it was under severe pressure, despite a short reaction time. Evidently, it was both J&K and Sri Lanka, which witnessed some of the fastest and most successful limited adjustments by tactical commanders. The modifications on vehicles, weapons, battalion organisation, use of captured equipment, local militia, etc. were attempted in both these areas. J&K is also the only region which witnessed revolutionary changes in the form of LoC Anti-Infiltration Obstacle System and RR battalions at the strategic and organisational levels.

The assessment also indicates that the experience of the army in Sri Lanka contributed to the subsequent operations in J&K. However, the process of learning from the experience in Sri Lanka was constrained by the inability to formally circulate a structured analysis of lessons learnt, which is borne by the fact that some of the adaptations followed a reactive, rather than a proactive course yet again in J&K. This was especially true in case of battalions, which had not served in Sri Lanka, prior to their induction into J&K.

Conclusion

An assessment of empirical evidence of strategic, organisational and operational changes in CI operations suggests the need to go beyond the existing framework and analyse change as relevant in the Indian context. It further highlights the difference between military change in a conventional environment and that in CI operations. Military change, both major and limited, clearly displays an evolutionary character, as compared to technology-inspired revolutionary changes in conventional warfare.

The challenges to successful military change reinforce the need to overcome existing limitations and weaknesses in the Indian system. While some of these suggest faster and better informed decision-making, others yet again bring out the need for empowering the officer cadre by limiting the curbs on information through a more mature declassification policy and documenting lessons from past conflicts.

The continued reliance on generalists has not facilitated change management. The book recommends professional capability-based human resource policies, which facilitate greater specialisation and continuity in decision-making.

NOTES

1. These changes are referred to as disruptive. See Theo Farrell, Frans Osinga and James A. Russell (eds.), *Military Adaptation in Afghanistan*, Stanford University Press, Stanford, 2013, pp. 6-7.

2. See *Doctrine for Sub Conventional Operations (DSCO)*, Integrated Headquarters of Ministry of Defence (Army), Headquarters Army Training Command, Shimla, December 2006, p. 22.
3. See "PM's address to the Annual Conference of DGPs/IGPs of States and UTs", Prime Minister of India, October 6, 2005, at http://pmindia.gov.in/speech-details.php?nodeid=201 (Accessed April 21, 2014); "Action Plan for Naxal-hit Districts Soon: Chidambaram", *The Times of India*, August 4, 2010, at http://timesofindia.indiatimes.com/india/Action-plan-for-Naxal-hit-districts-soon-Chidambaram/articleshow/6256386.cms (Accessed April 21, 2014).
4. See S. Kalyanaraman, "Major Lessons from Operation Pawan for Future Regional Stability Operations", *Journal of Defence Studies*, 6 (3), p. 37, at http://idsa.in/jds/6_3_2012_Major LessonsfromOperationPawanforFutureRegionalStabilityOperations_SKalyanaraman (Accessed April 11, 2014)
5. The inclusion of Dos and Don'ts as part of the Armed Forces Special Powers Act was a result of a judgement by the Supreme Court after a case was filed challenging the constitutional validity of the Act. Some inquiries into alleged human rights violations also followed pressure created by locals in the area of operations.
6. For a debate on the challenges of specialisation in the army, see: Anit Mukherjee, "Facing Future Challenges: Defence Reforms in India", *RUSI Journal*, 156 (5), October/November 2011, pp. 32-33.
7. For importance of informed decision-making, see: Josy Joseph, "It Takes Intellectual Capital for Security in this Century: Admiral James Starvridis", *The Times of India*, April 23, 2014, at http://m.timesofindia.com/home/opinion/interviews/It-takes-intellectual-capital-for-security-in-this-century-Admiral-James-Stavridis/articleshow/34081479.cms (Accessed May 01, 2014).
8. Brig. P.S. Mann, "Conduct of Junior Leaders in Counterinsurgency Operations", *USI Journal*, CXLI (584), April-June 2011, at http://www.usiofindia.org/Article/?pub=Journal&pubno =584&ano=821 (Accessed November 20, 2013).
9. The army did establish temporary divisional-level training schools, however, a formal structure came up in the form of the CIJW School in 1970.
10. Ashok K. Mehta, "India's Counterinsurgency Campaign in Sri Lanka", in Sumit Ganguly and David Fidler (eds.), *India and Counterinsurgency: Lessons Learned*, Routledge, New York, 2009, p. 170.
11. General V.P. Malik, *Kargil: From Surprise to Victory*, Harper Collins, New Delhi, 2006, p. 289.
12. Ibid., p. 285.
13. Ibid.
14. For a detailed analysis of the problem, read Anit Mukherjee, No. 6, p. 34.
15. Based on the author's personal experience in the area of operations.
16. Based on inputs by a former senior officer in the Division.
17. See S. Kalyanaraman, No. 4, p. 45.
18. Ibid., p. 46.
19. Harinder Baweja and Nitin Gokhale, "General Action", *Tehelka*, February 26, 2005, at http://archive.tehelka.com/story_main10.asp?filename=ts022605Genaral_action.asp&id=1 (Accessed April 15, 2014).

PART III

Analysing Military Change

9

Contextualising Military Change

The process of change, be it in the military, or as part of the corporate world, tends to remain a challenge. In many ways, organisations are similar to living organisms. They tend to develop peculiar characteristics, which gives them a distinct character. This makes the task of formulating a universal antidote for overcoming stagnation fraught with danger, especially for militaries, given their rigid structure, which more often than not resist any attempt at change. This duality of challenge, given the *inherent resistance to change* and *absence of a common framework* to undertake its implementation, highlights the reason why militaries often fail to evolve over a period of time. The absence of a systemic method or a standard operating procedure, something militaries are comfortable with, makes the very idea of change an anathema. Even when an endeavour is made, limited past experience, absence of a scientific methodology and a firm belief in the dictum, "If it ain't broke, don't fix it", constrain efforts to set change in motion.

Relating Lessons from the Corporate World

Over the years, there have been far greater attempts at analysing the theory, concept, process and successful implementation of change management in the corporate world, rather than the military domain. This is understandable, given the relative ease of analysing success and failure in the corporate world. The bottom-line approach and its associated processes create case studies with feverish frequency. These case studies, when taken up by management schools, become part of a large database, which provides an objective and rational basis for drawing relevant conclusions. This is further facilitated by the relative transparency of processes, systems, financial data and decision-making. In many ways, this very transparency and accountability in terms of bottom-line success ensures that a product or even a company does not survive unless it evolves successfully. This assessment is borne by the harsh reality of data.

Foster and Kaplan indicate that *Forbes* published its first top 100 companies list in 1917. By 1987, 61 of these had ceased to exist. Of the 39, just 18 were a part of the top 100. However, even these 18 earned 20 per cent less than the overall market during this period.[1] The Standard & Poor (S&P) top 500 list underwent a similar trajectory. From the 1957 list, a mere 74 survived by 1997. Of these, only 12 outperformed the S&P index over the same period.[2] According to the authors, the lifecycle of 65 years had further come down to 10 years by 1998, clearly reflecting the increasing challenge of a disconnect between a change in market dynamics and the transformative process in companies concerned. They relate this inability to change to a "cultural lock-in". The inability of a corporation to change its culture leads to rigidity and this affects its flexibility and innovativeness.[3]

This reality clearly reflects the inability of top-notch companies to adapt to change, despite attracting the best managerial talent, given the position of pride they hold in the job market. If this is the prevailing reality of private companies, could the state of armies be any different? It is unlikely to be so. And this is despite the fact that the factors which influence the success of armies and corporate entities are different. This is because a number of managerial processes that underline management of change are similar, as are the impediments. A number of factors related to organisational theory apply in both cases, which influence the way in which large entities behave and react. External factors, though very different in their nature, do impact in the form of drivers, which initiate change. A brief look at the types of change in the corporate world further reinforces this reality. Here, organisational change has been classified as: revolutionary versus evolutionary; discontinuous versus continuous; episodic versus continuous; transformational versus transactional; strategic versus operational; and total system versus local option.[4] These terms could very well describe the nature of change witnessed in armies across the world.

Despite these seemingly telling similarities, the unique situation that armies find themselves in makes the process of change and its evaluation a challenge. Unlike the private sector, where corporate battles are fought and won on a regular basis, the real test of military change for an army, or at times even the cause if its initiation is in the form of a conflict, may not happen in the life and times of a soldier. As a result, the declining frequency of wars, no longer test the efficacy of change in militaries. Even if they do not evolve, their failure is a reality that is embedded in the cosy atmosphere of mediocrity that remains busy fighting past wars. Militaries also survive as they are state enterprises, which function on state funding. They are therefore guaranteed a certain minimum infusion of money, which caters for administrative expenditure and modernisation needs. Since they perform the critical task of ensuring an atmosphere which allows every other private and public enterprise to function, their role remains largely uncontested within certain parameters of acceptability.

Even as it is a challenge to measure the failure to change, it is equally difficult to assess its success. As a result, a military which may remain mired in the past, but triumphs against a weak adversary, internal or external, might be seen as a modern and transformative force, despite obvious limitations. The crushing defeat of the forces of Saddam Hussain during the Second Gulf War was hailed for the clinical efficiency of the US Armed Forces. The implementation of a superior strategy, recognition of brilliant military leadership and network-centric warfare, all pointed towards a revolution in military affairs. However, this assessment was soon revised when the US Armed Forces faced the challenge of fighting a sub-conventional adversary in the very same country, as part of a military continuum.

Similarly, even during the absence of a conflict, the inability to provide viable military alternatives to an elected government in order to take on prevailing challenges, may not be an obvious failure to evolve, but is certainly a limitation that could or should have been taken into consideration as part of the process of military change. The Indian Armed Forces were arraigned along the border for a period just short of a year during Operation Parakram in 2001, in the immediate aftermath of the Pakistan-sponsored attack on the Parliament. However, it was evident that the requisite military alternatives needed to circumvent the nuclear deterrence prevailing between India and Pakistan were constrained and stunted by the lack of viable military options. It was equally relevant that the national decision-making structure had not evolved a grand strategy which could overcome such situations and simultaneously help create capacities within the armed forces to implement it. It was this limitation that gave rise to the Cold Start option thereafter in 2004, though at the initiative of the army and seemingly without the national security apparatus on board.

This presents a challenge for military practitioners. Even if they have the desired intent and the will to undertake change, it is difficult to assess the correctness of their selected path. This carries within its ambit a dangerous debilitating factor. In a hierarchical organisation like the army, the difficulty to assess poor change management could lead to its unimpeded implementation. This is unlike the corporate world, where companies receive regular consumer feedback or are affected by a declining bottom line. In an army, the absence of either quantifiable or realistic feedback could create a false sense of success and effectiveness. This situation can further aggravate, if policymakers in the government do not have the necessary expertise to assess the effectiveness of military change or a team of specialists who can independently validate ongoing changes. It is further affected by the absence of strategic guidance, which provides the directives for implementing changes by all organs of the state, including the army.

This reinforces the need for creating and maintaining an organisational culture that supports this process at a number of levels. First, it should provide the environment that encourages innovation and creativity. Second, the organisation should have the inherent strength to throw up professional military leadership. Third, this leadership should be integrated into the national decision-making authority. Fourth, the national decision-making authority should have access to expertise that can validate military decisions. Last, a feedback mechanism should be able to provide the necessary inputs to allow course corrections and validation of changes undertaken. Amongst these, the most difficult and important factor remains the first, which deals with creation of the requisite organisational culture within the army to create an environment that allows the incubation and growth of ideas, as also its implementation.

Does Existing Theory Explain Military Change?

The first chapter dealt in detail with contrasting and contending theories and frameworks for better understanding military change. The arguments put forth by authors based on different periods of history as illustrative case studies make a strong statement with compelling logic. However, these tend to get challenged when applied to periods of history other than those cited by authors. Therefore, this book specifically relates to the case studies that have been taken up for assessment.

The assessment of military change commences with its very definition. Over a period of time, either references to innovation or more specifically military change have been defined by a number of authors. The definitions of Posen, Rosen and Farrell in the larger context of conventional conflicts and Afghanistan as well as the one suggested by Grissom have been quoted in the opening chapter. While I have employed the framework of Farrell in the past in isolation to earlier papers, using it as a combination in the context of both conventional and sub-conventional conflicts makes for a challenge. This reinforces Grissom's view that even as certain key factors are common from the perspectives offered by different authors, no single work completely exemplifies an understanding of the phenomenon in its entirety. This leads to the understanding that *first*, attempts to narrow the definition or even the understanding of military change can potentially lead to a failure to understand it in its entirety. *Second*, since most armies are likely to fight the challenge of both conventional and sub-conventional conflicts concurrently, or at least be prepared for both simultaneously, analysing any one of them in isolation could lead to flawed conclusions. *Third*, while change often tends to get associated with major shifts in the form of innovations in the conventional domain, the inclusion of sub-conventional warfare will invariably lead to the less glamorous evolutionary adaptions into the mainstream (as emphasised by the section on counterinsurgency warfare). These factors get further elaborated upon based on an assessment of specific aspects that emerged as part of the survey in the concluding chapter.

Posen's theory of change – emanating from failure, driven by mavericks and supported by the government – is only partially relatable to shifts noticed after the 1962 Sino-Indian War, since this was neither initiated nor implemented by mavericks. The changes as a result of the 1975 reforms followed a military victory instead and were yet again carried forward by the senior hierarchy of the army. His emphasis on change being driven by civilian intervention is also questionable since the professional content of most changes in the Indian context came from the senior military leadership. Moreover, in case of counterinsurgency (CI) operations, to a large extent in case of evolutionary shifts, it was a bottom-up approach initiated by tactical commanders.

Rosen's understanding that armies are unlikely to innovate in peacetime, unless it is an act of civilian intervention, does not necessarily relate to the Indian context. The thrust on mechanisation and employment of mobile warfare was a military initiated reform. Similarly, the raising of the Rashtriya Rifles (RR), as well as the artificial obstacle system along the Line of Control (LoC), was yet again influenced more by the army. However, in each of the cases, these changes could not have reached fruition without the support of the government, as has emerged clearly from the case studies. Rosen's contention of innovation being driven by the senior military hierarchy is reinforced by most case studies where military change was a top-down process. In case of CI operations, the reverse is equally true, wherein change was initiated by tactical leaders, even though in certain cases, it was ultimately implemented in a top-down fashion, as seen from the case studies analysed earlier. Rosen also posits that innovation is unlikely to take place during wars. This is true for major changes and is reinforced in the Indian context; however, yet again, CI operations will almost always buck this trend. Given the protracted nature of conflicts, it is more likely to witness innovations, adaptions and emulation being applied during the course of a conflict.

The debate over military culture is instructive. Dima Adamsky emphasises its importance in relation to military innovation, especially when compared to technology. Similarly, Williamson Murray links its impact to the ability to change, or perhaps even evolve over a period of time. Murray relates cultural emphasis to aspects like professional military education, intellectualism of the officer cadre and relevance of learning historical lessons in order to provide the right direction to military change.

The understanding of military or strategic culture as part of organisational culture and its influence on military affairs is also reinforced by Rosen, Nagl, Johnston and Gray, as discussed in the first chapter. The impact of strategic culture is undisputed. This is also evident from the evolutionary trends of Indian military behaviour both in CI operations and conventional wars. However, it also emerges simultaneously that strategic culture functions more as underlying environmental condition which shapes the behaviour of an organisation over a protracted period of time, rather than directly driving change. Therefore, it would be more appropriate to see strategic culture as an enabler or shaper for military change instead of a driver.

Nagl makes some interesting observations on the relevance of doctrines and its impact, especially in case of CI operations. He feels that doctrines tend to make actions inflexible, which can lead to military defeat. In order to support his prognosis, he takes the case study of British and US experiences in Malaya and Vietnam, respectively. It is challenging to relate this factor in the Indian context, especially since the first formal doctrine for sub-conventional operations was only released in 2006, despite the army having been involved in such operations since 1955. It is all the more relevant because, some suggestions claim doctrine as a driver for initiating change. And since, at times it tends to be used interchangeably with strategy, its importance is further amplified. In the Indian context, with specific reference to CI operations, the impact of a formal doctrine has been limited. At the local level, the relevance of standard operating procedures (SOPs), which are often derivates of an operational guideline tend to have greater significance. However, this does not unduly constrain the operational freedom of junior leaders, which is evident from the nature of tactical operations that have been conducted over a period of time, as also from the relative success of the army in this field. In a way this reinforces Nagl's contention. Interestingly, India has not had a very strong doctrinal culture in the conventional sphere as well. It is often a challenge to define the doctrinal underpinnings of the army over the post-independence period. Yet, at times, it has been noted that innovation at the strategic level has remained limited in the past. This leads to the observation that in addition to the doctrinal culture of an army, its organisational and strategic culture possibly has greater influence on its behaviour over a period of time, as discussed earlier.

Nagl also indicates the importance of bottom-up feedback and a top-down doctrine. In the Indian case, this is indeed the case, wherein considerable tactical lessons have translated into doctrinal guidelines over a period of time and find mention in the army's doctrine.

Further, Nagl links changes to the organisational culture of various armies. He goes on to give examples of the British and US armies in this regard to reinforce the point. Janine Davidson contrasts this with the relevance and importance of learning cultures as a critical driver for military change instead. Her relation of learning and teaching cultures comes up as important constituents instead. Davidson's prognosis cannot be disputed, as the case studies clearly indicate that certain limitations in India's context could have been influenced negatively by constraints in this regard. This is especially relevant in case of higher defence management in case of both conventional and CI operations. In an attempt to reinforce the argument, views of the environment through a survey were taken, with some of these issues being thrown up in the form of questions. Predictably, the conclusions that emerge reinforce limitations in relation to the learning processes that have been highlighted earlier.

The focus of the section on conventional warfare is on revolutionary change for the simple reason that it is this form of change which is more difficult to conceive and implement. Therefore, its understanding and possibly even the reasons for its failure remain critical. However, as the section on CI operations indicates, operational changes, even though they may not be revolutionary in nature, can potentially make a significant impact. These evolutionary changes can also lay the groundwork for subsequent changes which may well be revolutionary in nature. A more detailed assessment of military change in the Indian CI context helps elaborate these factors through a comparative analysis of these changes in relation to current literature on the subject.

The framework applied to analyse military change in CI operations reinforces certain facets of existing research, even as it highlights important differences as well (see Part II – Military Change in Counterinsurgency). The section reinforces a number of parameters highlighted by Farrell et al. in their study of the Afghanistan insurgency.[5] These include:

- Importance of operational factors to military change in CI operations.

- Adaptation can cumulatively contribute to innovation or major changes.
- Inability to adapt at tactical levels can lead to failure at strategic levels.
- Significance of change is not the basis for innovation or major changes.
- Operational threats are the most important driver for military change.

However, the book finds significant differences in some other areas, which relate more to contextual variations. In the case of India, especially when compared to Afghanistan, where an international coalition of forces has been employed, the role of the army has been distinct in comparison. The Indian Army has been deployed for such operations in a domestic context, with the exception of Operation Pawan in Sri Lanka, for prolonged durations, with the aim of facilitating reconciliation between the estranged population and the state. At no stage of the conflict in India, the army or the government had the option of withdrawing, as the International Security Assistance Force (ISAF) largely did in Afghanistan in 2014, and as the Indian Army could in the case of Sri Lanka in 1990. The differences in local conditions prevalent in India vis-à-vis Afghanistan affect not only the application of force, but also the ability of the military to adapt to change.

Farrell et al. identify strategy, force generation, and/or change to military plans and operations as the types of military change in Afghanistan, while the Indian example suggests these as strategic, organisational and operational in nature. As part of the Afghanistan example, force generation includes force levels, equipment, training, and doctrine, as highlighted earlier; however, these are best classified as part of strategic or operational change based on the nature and level of adaptation witnessed. Military plans, yet again can either be a part of strategic or operational change, depending on the level, nature and scale of change envisaged.

The book reinforces Ferrell's conclusion that the sliding scale of military adaptation is valid; however, its components, manifestation and impact as a result of implementation do have a variance in the Indian context. The importance of shapers mentioned by Farrell plays a marginal role in CI operations in India. This is partly a result of factors like alliance politics, civil-military relations and domestic politics having a limited impact on military functions in CI operations, given broad-based political consensus on internal challenges, in the past. While these factors, do play a role in decision-making in a generic context, however, specifically with reference to change in CI operations, their impact has not been substantive. For example, the debate on the Armed Forces Special Powers Act (AFSPA) 1990, in Jammu and Kashmir (J&K), witnessed divergent stands by the state government and the army.[6] This may have had a marginal psychological influence on soldiers; however, the position of the army has consistently been endorsed by the central government, thereby limiting any impact and neutralising constraints on operational efficiency. In Manipur, under strong pressure of public opinion, the central district of Imphal was removed from the areas declared disturbed.[7] This virtually barred the army from operating there. However, even in this case, the impact of the move cannot qualify as a major adverse influence on the effectiveness of the army, since readjustment of forces is often carried out as a routine function. The case of Sri Lanka could also be a possible example of the impact of domestic politics, given the influence of Tamil politics. While Tamil sentiment in Tamil Nadu and its political impact are politically relevant factors,[8] these did not place constraints on the military conduct of operations of the Indian Peace Keeping force (IPKF). In Punjab, despite a politically charged atmosphere, the decision to send in the army into the Golden Temple is yet another example of the limited impact of domestic politics in the fight against terrorism.

Unlike the army, domestic politics can potentially have a major impact on the conduct of operations of police and paramilitary forces, which come under and function in close association with the state administration.

The concept of shapers is also relevant to India, however, with some differences. *First,* political directives act as drivers, even as political influence in an area of operations acts as a shaper as part of environmental pressure. Nehru's directive and the change in role in Sri Lanka were both drivers for change. However, political pressures as a result of local politics in states like J&K and Manipur often created an environment, which influence the actions of the army without driving them directly. *Second,* environmental pressure is also a driver in cases where its focused impact is able to drive change. However, in all other cases it remains a shaper. This manifests in terms of public opinion, often voiced through the media. It has in the past impacted decision-making, as is evident from the evolutionary policy of the CI doctrine over a period of time. However, this factor has also been a driver in the case of amendment of AFSPA, which witnessed the formal inclusion of Dos and Don'ts as binding guidelines.[9] *Third*, unlike the Afghanistan example, even technology drives change only in certain cases, while for the others, it acts more as a shaper, providing the environment for facilitating change. For example, the establishment of the LoC fence was driven by operational threats; however, the availability of technology shaped the complementary utilisation of aids like sensors and other surveillance devices.

While operational threats remain the most important driver, as Farrell found, technology is also relevant, though to a limited extent. This also reinforces the fact that unlike conventional operations, it is more difficult to create a framework for assessing CI operations in the context of military change, give the peculiarities of each region and country.

In light of the assessment of competing frameworks, military change can best be defined, especially if it has to deal with both conventional and CI threats as:

> Military change represents an attempt at developing a significantly more effective approach to existing or future military challenges.

The definition merely outlines the intent, though it does not elaborate upon the associated factors, which can help complete its understanding. In the absence of these factors, any definition remains open to varying interpretations. The following part of this chapter elaborates upon some of these factors in more specific terms. This is derived from case studies analysed in previous chapters and other suitable examples that reinforce the assessment.

Drivers of Military Change

Drivers of military change can be external or internal to an organisation. Amongst the most important and common drivers is the operational or strategic environment. This shapes the nature of challenges faced by a country in ways that necessitate the need for changes in military strategy. Most cases witness the precipitation of such changes as a reaction to developing circumstances. However, under ideal conditions, leaders should be able to assess emerging contours in order to reduce the time needed for visualising and implementing changes. This differentiates visionary leaders from the others who tend to remain reactive in their approach to military change.

Technology is yet another factor which can drive military change. However, the availability of technology is not a guarantee of its effective employment for bringing about change. It is accompanied by the scientific ability of a country to harness it and further drive military use. Development of technology should also be a financially viable proposition, as its implementation must retain or ideally reduce the budgetary limitations, which are bound to balance costs and effects. Technology must further be accompanied by the vision to employ it to create substantial advantage against the adversary. Unless all these factors are fulfilled, the advent of technology will remain in the realms of demonstrative relevance, without the practicality of accompanying implementation. For example, the concept of network-centric warfare: The army has clearly indicated its desire to become a network-centric force.[10] However, for a number of years, despite this clearly enunciated desire, while certain advancements have been made, the army and the armed forces are still far from achieving this capability. Further, given the strain likely to be felt to pursue modernisation, the ability to achieve this capability, for armed forces of the size maintained by India, seems highly unlikely in the foreseeable future.

Strategy and doctrine can potentially serve as viable drivers of military change. A shift in a country's or even an army's doctrine can change the guiding principles for the conduct of warfare. However, change in doctrines is not a prerequisite for incorporating military change. Even as the doctrine remains the same, a strategic shift, which deals with a radically different method of dealing with an adversary, can bring about a military change. These two factors are closely interlinked. As a result, for real change to be realised, strategic changes, which represent a more functional aspect of change, become more important than doctrinal shifts alone. This is especially relevant in the absence of accompanying strategic changes. This can be best explained with an example related to India and its army. Over the years, the army gradually made a shift towards deterrence by punishment from defensive deterrence, with reference to Pakistan. However, in the absence of a viable military capability to follow up a likely serious provocation, India's doctrine of punishment by deterrence remained inadequate. However, the unveiling of "Cold Start" strategy, irrespective of its eventual viability which has been debated in academic circles, was an attempt to provide the doctrine with the necessary efficacy. Cold Start has been referred by some as a doctrine. However, its elements suggest that it was a strategic initiative, which was a follow-up of the doctrine unveiled by the army in 2004.

In contrast, the impact of doctrines and strategies while still important could be less relevant in CI conditions, given the peculiar condition of each CI area and the challenge of creating an area-specific doctrine or strategy. Their importance as guidelines however remains a shaper which impacts the overall conduct of operations.

With reference to CI operations, the relevance of political directions could also emerge as a driver, through its impact has been seen only in relation to changing goals. This, if and when relevant to conventional threats, could also emerge as a driver.

As discussed earlier, strategic culture often referred to as a driver emerges more in the form of an underlying guideline which influences the manner in which militaries tend to operate. Therefore, even as its relevance and importance is critical, classifying it is as a driver may not best describe its application.

The debate on learning processes has also been dealt with earlier in the chapter. These in many ways help create the military or strategic culture that makes armies operate, function and think in a more scientific and cogent manner, which in itself facilitates the process of change.

Who Drives Military Change?

There are different perspectives on the source of military change. To a large extent it differs from country to country, based on the security decision-making structure and prevalent culture. This brings in the vital and relevant aspect of civil military relations into play and the inclusiveness of the armed forces and more specifically the army in making and influencing decisions related to national security.

Varying perspectives on the issue have already been discussed earlier in the book. One view is that change is driven by the government with support from mavericks.[11] There is also a view that military change is influenced by the government along with the senior hierarchy of the armed forces.[12] The former option is a possible scenario wherein the decision-makers in the government are willing to break protocol and the strictly hierarchical structure of the armed forces to directly encourage and seek feedback from selected officers. Amongst the few instances, wherein this can be related to the Indian Army, is the period when Lt Gen, B.M. Kaul was closely associated with Prime Minister Jawaharlal Nehru just prior to the 1962 Sino-Indian War. However, even during this period, there was no substantial change that they could effectively implement to change the army. Conversely, they are often accused of not only subverting the military system of functioning but to some degree, responsible for the eventual defeat. This experience could have well discouraged the political leadership from bypassing senior military leadership, as is evident since then. This has led to a more predictable approach as suggested by Rosen, wherein the professional advice of the senior military hierarchy has been instrumental in the government's approach to matters military. In addition to the case studies discussed in the previous chapters, the influence of the army on political decision-making with regard to withdrawal from the Siachen Glacier is a case in point.[13] The only limitation that deserves further reinforcement is the need to institutionalise the role of the armed forces in higher defence management of the country to ensure a more structured approach to security matters.

In addition to employment of these institutional systems for decision-making, including for driving military change, the impact of personalities and their ability to hasten or push through reforms cannot be understated. The role of Sundarji has been underscored earlier. Similarly, it is equally relevant to highlight the response of the political leadership. The speed and scope of change can be, as has been illustrated in the past, path-breaking, with major implications for the defence forces and security of the country.

More specifically in the case of CI operations, given that change often emerges from the tactical level, it can be driven by junior leaders who adapt to the operational challenges, thereby creating the necessary bottom-up capillary action for initiating major changes.

Pathways to Military Change

The assessment of case studies in both CI and conventional domains suggests different pathways that have been taken or can be taken to implement military change. Farrell and Terriff highlight these as *innovation*, *adaptation* and *emulation*.[14] The Indian Army has experienced all three pathways in the course of its experience with change. While Mizoram and Nagaland witnessed emulation of a number of British practices in CI operations, a much larger number of adaptations were undertaken at the tactical level. Innovation has been more difficult to come by, however, examples like the RR, even though they may have drawn from past experience of 'I' battalions and Assam Rifles, was a major change. Similarly, the mechanisation of the army after the 1975 reforms, was also an equally substantial shift in the conventional domain.

The Indian experience in CI operations suggests that there is high possibility of adaptations evolving further and finally emerging as innovations, given the scale, impact and substantial shift they are able to bring about in operations. The same is not as relevant in the conventional domain as, the tactical battlefield dominates CI operations and remains the focal point of operations. Conversely, large-scale victories are shaped by strategies, in the absence of which, predictability could well become the norm in war.

Direction of Military Change

Military change in the conventional sphere remains essentially a top-down action, driven by the senior military leadership, duly supported by the political establishment. This entails evolution of military plans from a military strategy, which flows from a military doctrine. The doctrine itself is a derivative of the national security strategy, which could well be a part of the grand strategy. Some of these steps may be omitted, or others added; however, this is primarily the approach to implementation of directions in the army. As the process suggests, there is little scope for a bottom-up approach in this format of decision-making. The only exception to this format could be the impact of bottom-up feedback to orders or changes, which could result in course correction over a period of time.

This top-down approach is challenged in case of CI operations. As has been illustrated in the case studies, a large number of operational changes are bottom-up in CI operations. These may not fit into the classical definition of military innovation; however, as has been seen in the Indian context and in recent times in Afghanistan, these bottom-up operational changes can become a catalyst for major changes and evolve over a period of time to develop into innovations. Therefore, for armies which face a duality of military challenges, to include CI as well as conventional threats, the direction of change could vary under different circumstances and conditions. This further suggests that a strictly rigid mindset, which only expects and directs change from the top, is liable to fail in CI operations. The challenges faced by the army as a result of this very rigid mindset during its initial years in CI operations is a case in point. This possibility also suggests that the conditions and organisational culture of an army must allow and facilitate the churning of ideas at the tactical level, as also be ready to imbibe the same if it indicates the potential for larger and more effective shifts.

Scale of Change

The impact that military change brings about can also be influenced by its scale. Change that is organisation wide is likely to have a far greater impact than the one which is limited to a small section within the army. It is also likely though not as must that large-scale changes tend to be revolutionary in nature as compared to small changes which are generally evolutionary.

A look at some of the case studies discussed reinforces this trend. From the perspective of the CI campaign in J&K, the creation of the artificial obstacle system was a large-scale change, as also revolutionary in terms of the impact it had. Conversely, modifications to weapons and strengthening of vehicles were small scale changes, which were locally engineered.

Level of Change

When military change is discussed and analysed, it tends to be equated with strategic changes. This is primarily because more often than not, strategic changes are revolutionary and have a major impact on an organisation and the way it plans to fight. It is also for this reason that the case studies in the section on conventional changes are attempts at major military change. Conversely, CI operations are impacted to a large extent by operational shifts and changes. It is therefore not surprising that Theo Farrell and Terry Terriff focus largely on strategic issues in their book, *The*

Sources of Military Change. However, while dealing with the CI conditions in Afghanistan, Farrell provides a definition which includes the operational aspects as well.

This experience is reinforced by case studies analysed in this book. For an army which must operate across a wide spectrum of conflict, to include both conventional and sub conventional operations, it is therefore important to consider and focus equally on changes at the strategic and operational levels. The tendency to merely look at military change as synonymous with strategic changes could lead to neglect of an equally important aspect of change management.

Type of Change

Military change manifests itself primarily in the form of evolutionary or revolutionary change. This is not different from the corporate world, or for that matter in the literature that analyses changes in that sector.[15] It is also reiterated by Burke that most changes continue to remain evolutionary rather than revolutionary.[16] Therefore, in co-relation, it is not surprising that most changes in a military structure are also evolutionary in nature and the challenges to bring about revolutionary changes remain significant. The preponderance of evolutionary changes is possibly a case of stating the obvious. It is possibly more relevant to analyse the impact of leaders and organisational culture, which as indicated earlier is closely linked with an army's strategic culture on the type of change.

NOTES

1. Richard Foster and Sarah Kaplan, *Creative Destruction: Why Companies That Are Build to Last Underperform the Market – And How to Successfully Transform Them*, Doubleday, New York, 2001, pp. 7-8.
2. Ibid., p. 8.
3. Ibid., p. 11.
4. W. Warner Burke, *Organisational Change: Theory and Practice*, Sage Publications, New Delhi, 2012, p. 22.
5. Theo Farrell, Frans Osinga and James A. Russell (eds.), *Military Adaptation in Afghanistan*, Stanford University Press, Stanford, 2013, pp. 1-23.
6. See Muddasir Ali, "Omar Hits out at Army Stand on AFSPA", *Greater Kashmir*, February 23, 2014, at http://www.greaterkashmir.com/news/2014/Feb/23/omar-hits-out-at-army-stand-on-afspa-63.asp (Accessed April 16, 2014).
7. Siddharth Varadarajan, "Partial Lifting of Act May Not Help", *The Hindu*, August 13, 2004, at http://www.hindu.com/2004/08/13/stories/2004081307331100.htm (Accessed April 16, 2014).

8. Ashok K. Mehta, "India's Counterinsurgency Campaign in Sri Lanka", in Sumit Ganguly and David Fidler (eds.), *India and Counterinsurgency: Lessons Learned*, Routledge, New York, 2009, p 168.
9. *Naga People's Movement, of Human ... vs Union of India*, Supreme Court of India, November 27, 1997, at http://indiankanoon.org/doc/1072165/ (Accessed on March 31, 2014).
10. It was designated as a Key Result Area by successive Chiefs of the Army Staff, including Gen. J. J. Singh in 2005.
11. Barry Posen, *The Sources of Military Doctrine: France, Britain and Germany Between the World Wars*, Cornell University Press, Ithaca, 1984, p. 241.
12. Stephen Peter Rosen, *Winning the Next War: Innovation and the Modern Military*, Cornell University Press, Ithaca, 1991, p. 21.
13. Siddhartha Srivastava, "India's Army Digs in over Siachen", *Asia Times*, November 16, 2006, at http://www.atimes.com/atimes/South_Asia/HK16Df01.html (Accessed December 18, 2015).
14. Theo Farrell and Terry Terriff (eds.), *The Sources of Military Change: Culture, Politics, Technology*, Lynne Rienner Publishers, Boulder, 2002, p. 6.
15. See W. Warner Burke, No. 4, pp. 73-98.
16. Ibid. Burke mentions a percentage of 95 for evolutionary changes, which essentially indicates the preponderance of such changes in any organisation.

10

Concluding Observations

In order to understand military change better, and with a degree of objectivity, this book essentially follows a case-study model. The case studies not only provide the basis for analysing specific changes undertaken by the army in the past but also give an insight into the procedures and processes that accompanied them. Consequently, certain takeaways emerge clearly in terms of the realities of military change in the Indian context, as also factors which drive it and facilitate the process. If these issues were summarised, they would fall under two distinct categories – from the point of view of limitations noticed or strengths identified. This in part relates to the army, which is the predominant agency driving change management in the sub-conventional domain, with limited influence from the political leadership and bureaucracy, since most changes tend to remain operational and tactical in nature. However, in case of conventional threats, while the army remains the principle agency for implementing change, the influence of strategic direction and political support goes beyond the organisational influence of the army. Further, effectiveness and capacity building are also influenced by organisations which are part of the national security architecture and are not necessarily army-centric. As part of the concluding observations, I intend to highlight and at places reinforce the role of the army and the overall national security architecture, given their relevance for successful military change.

Change must ideally flow from the national security structure of a country, irrespective of the specific organisations involved, which tend to vary from country to country, and across systems. The case studies related to conventional change suggest that military reform was essentially spearheaded by the army, though critically with support from the political establishment. However, irrespective of the resultant impact, the tendency to undertake such major and often transformational shifts without the benefit of a clearly enunciated national security strategy, a defence situational review, a defence strategy or even a joint strategy for the armed forces creates conditions that perforce tend to force the armed forces to function with an inadequate understanding of a national perspective on these issues. This often leads to contradictions as a result of single-service doctrines or strategies, which do not necessarily carry the weight of the government behind them. This leads to a catch-22 situation, wherein not formulating a strategy or doctrine in the absence of a national strategy adversely affects functional efficiency, and introducing one in isolation produces at best a limited view of the subject. The circumstances created by these conditions limit the ability to plan and implement military change. The example of the so-called 'Cold Start' doctrine is a case in point, which has been highlighted previously.

India's stature and capability is undergoing a change. This is increasingly being accompanied by rising aspirations and expectations of India in the region. An assessment of the behaviour of major powers reveals that if there is one factor which all of them aspire to attain, it is the ability to remain proactive in their decision-making process. In other words, creating a capability to remain a step ahead of their adversaries. For this to become a reality in the sphere of military change, reactionary crisis management must cede space to proactive decision-making. This can only happen when decisions follow a well-orchestrated and planned course of action, which must flow from a clearly enunciated and formulated national assessment of threats, challenges and aims.[1] The absence of this function as an institutional process remains a constraint for both proactive decision-making and deliberate, considered and futuristic military change.

It has been highlighted repeatedly during the course of this study that military change as related to the army can no longer be a service-specific responsibility and function. This is evident by virtue of the role and function of joint service organisations like the Headquarters Integrated Defence Staff, Office of Chairman Chiefs of Staff Committee, Strategic Forces Command and Andaman and Nicobar Command. Some of these organisations have performed admirably despite the limitations of inadequate jointness and slow pace of reforms in this regard. However, even as these organisations are often analysed for enhancing their effectiveness, the absence of a Chief of Defence Staff (CDS) and the importance and criticality of an integrated Ministry of Defence (MoD), is often lost sight of. The continuation of service-specific thinking on change management is closely related to limitations within the armed forces, their not being integrated with the MoD and tri-services institutions not fully achieving the true potential of these organisational structures. The imperfection of these critical nodal structures ensures that future change management in a joint environment will either not fructify or follow parochial paths chartered by individual services, which will require both money and time to undo in the future. This is not a luxury defence of India can afford, especially given the delays in this regard that have already affected military change and the security environment in the region.

The next major recommendation also relates to the army and the national security architecture. The armed forces are undoubtedly the repository of professional military knowledge specifically in the context of operational issues. In relative terms and in all fairness, the political leadership cannot be equally aware of these concerns. However, this is not a situation that is unique to India alone. Yet, military change has taken place in a number of countries, especially in circumstances wherein different services hold vastly different views on issues under debate. The political leadership has displayed at critical junctures of the country's history that it has the ability and drive to take major decisions related to defence. However, this is constrained by two factors. *First*, there is an absence of a formal system to support the decision-making process. This can be corrected by an organisational structure of which the armed forces must become an integral part. *Second*, even when such structures are created, their employment often remains inadequate. This limits the ability of political leaders to take major decisions or function as the driving force behind such decisions. Change is less likely to come from new structures that get created, but more as a result of effective functioning of existing ones along with requisite restructuring that must accompany this process.

The limitations associated with the ability to conduct structural reforms are linked with the need to debate the same. An informed debate on such issues can only take place if related information is placed in public domain. There has been a tendency in the past to avoid public debate and discussion on important structural reforms. While strictly operational issues cannot be discussed openly, issues like restructuring of the MoD or the creation of CDS can and must form a part of public discourse. This must include declassification of past reports and studies on the subject to enable erudite opinions. This will also enhance accountability of the decision-making process. Further, it will ensure collective and cohesive decision making, as also limit the margin of error in case of major changes envisaged.

A large section of the book has been devoted to military change as related to sub-conventional operations. These operations relate to both defensive and offensive capability, with the latter alluding to striking terrorists beyond the national territory. As case studies quoted earlier suggest, offensive changes have been rare to come by, in comparison with defensive and reactionary ones. The establishment of a special forces command is a case in point. Since the responsibility of such operations is viewed only from a special forces perspective, the role of intelligence agencies and other supporting organisations within the country tends to get neglected. In reality, it is a whole-of-government effort. Military change in this regard must therefore flow from the national level and be accompanied by capability development of each of the agencies concerned, which will contribute to creation and implementation of this capability. This further reinforces the role of integrating the national strategic vision with each of the accompanying element, including the army.

The other part of the conclusion relates specifically to the army and its ability to undertake change. In addition to some of the conclusions and observations that have been flagged earlier, a survey was conducted amongst officers of the army, both serving and retired. This was kept independent of the previous analysis, which was based on case studies and their relation with organisational functioning and its effectiveness. As part of the survey, the options provided for each question were related to potential reasons for each factor that needed further investigation. While some of these emerged from the previous assessment, others were added to cover a wider spectrum of views that might be available. In order to receive the requisite feedback, a questionnaire was circulated to officers to elicit their response to issues related to military change, its contributing organisational culture and leadership.

The methodology adopted for seeking data was on the basis of a questionnaire created in Google Forms. This questionnaire was circulated through closed groups of serving and retired officers of the army. In addition, it was also sent to individual officers by email. This led to a total of 53 responses, which were analysed before arriving at an environmental view of factors related to military change. The benefit that the survey gave included anonymity of response, inputs from both serving and retired officers, views of a wide cross section, from different arms and services as well as service bracket. The responses were received from officers representing nine different arms and services, and their service bracket ranged from 9-39 years.

The survey was conducted within certain constraints, which limited the ability to create ideal conditions for receiving inputs. This included the inability to structure responses according to different segments like specific years of service, arms and services and regional representation amongst officers. The methodology adopted did not provide desirable flexibility due to the limited sample size, given constraints to approach officers in service. This affected the ability to relate the sample size to the complete pool of officers who could have possibly provided data. The inability to control responses during the stage of input was a limitation introduced due to electronic means of collection employed, rather than physical data collection, which is more reliable. However, despite these limitations, an attempt was made to collect adequate data to indicate opinions with a reasonable degree of accuracy and project trends, which are representative of overall thinking in the army.

The questions were focussed towards issues like strategic culture, professional military education (PME), tactical adaptation, strategic innovation, professional development of the officer cadre, challenges to military change, sources of military change and importance of specialisation. The conclusions that the survey suggests are self-explanatory and provide a clear indicator towards the steps that need to be initiated to better deal with military change in the army.

The first set of questions relate to India's military strategy. It is considered an important input for the study, since changes in strategy are important drivers for change. The questions also attempted to address the limitation of not necessarily having a written military strategy, though it is evident from the responses received from the officers that it is not necessarily difficult to discern the same, even if it is apparently not documented.

The first question related to the pace of evolution of India's military strategy. An overwhelming 81 per cent officers felt that the strategy was slow in its evolution. A mere 8 per cent saw it as fast evolving, while 9 per cent saw it as constant (see Chart 1). This clearly indicates the perceived pace of strategic changes in the Indian context, which as indicated earlier is one of the major drivers for military change. This implies that constraints have been placed on innovation due to the inability to evolve and respond to changing conditions and circumstances. It also reinforces the conclusion of the study that the army has played catch-up in terms of its strategic stance on the basis of challenges that were presented by the adversary.

A related question attempted to seek views of officers on how innovative was army's strategy (see Chart 2). This drew a similar response as the previous question, with an overwhelming 92 per cent indicating that the strategy remains predictable and a mere 2 per cent seeing it as innovative. This clearly reflects the inability of the army to bring about major changes in the perception of respondents, not merely in the domain of strategy, but also other factors, since the innovativeness needed to adapt to threats has remained limited in its conception and execution.

Despite attempts at coercive diplomacy through military posturing in the past, as witnessed during Operation Parakram and the Cold Start strategy, discussed earlier in the book, 57 per cent of the responders felt that the army's strategy remained defensive, while 26 per cent felt that it was offensive defence. 6 per cent saw it as offensive (see Chart 3). These indicators are quite clearly a collective perception of the army's response towards both Pakistan and China. While it is not feasible to analyse the specific reasons for the assessment, given that the questionnaire did not seek a country-specific answer, however, perceptions could have been influenced by different threat levels from the two countries.

Chart 1: Pace of Evolution of Army's Strategy

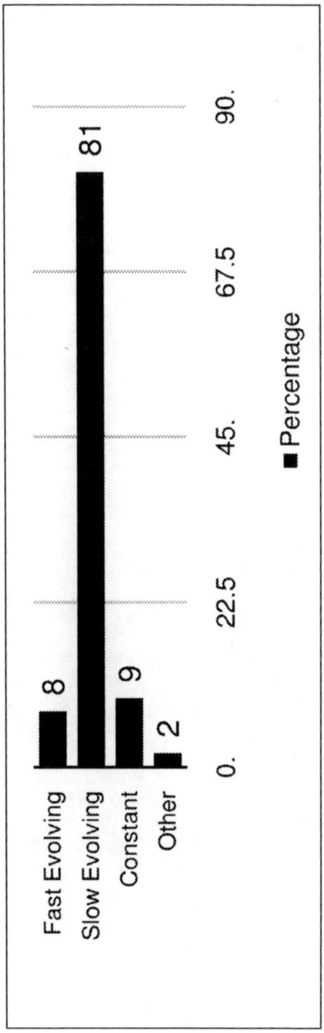

Chart 2: Innovation in Army Strategy

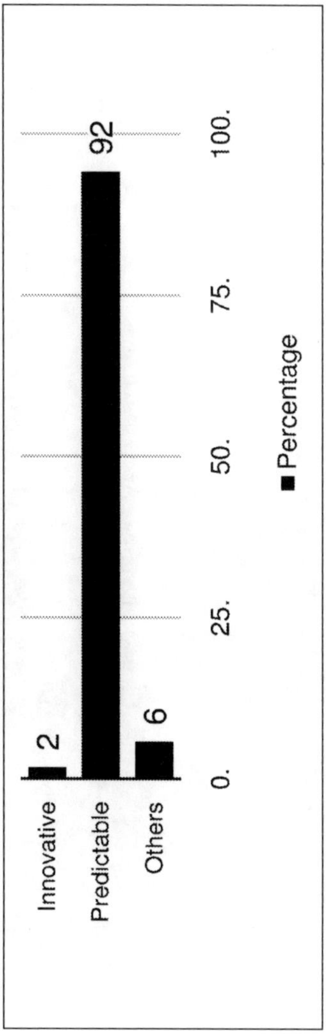

Chart 3: Nature of Army's Strategy

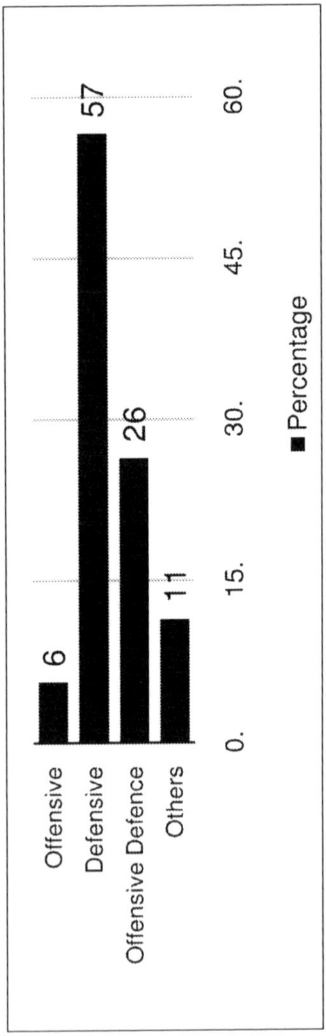

The question relating to the description of India's military strategy evoked mixed and interesting responses (see Chart 4). While 45 per cent indicated that the strategy is not documented but can be perceived, 34 per cent suggested that it is personality oriented and 16 per cent indicated that there was no strategy. This illustrates a case which may not be peculiar to the Indian Army alone, since a large number of countries and armies do not release their military strategies in the public domain. However, as this response suggests, it is possible to discern the same, at least for professionals, who are either a part of the system or follow it closely. The indication to personality oriented formulation of strategies, though not unique to the Indian Army, also raises the need for strengthening institutional mechanisms, which can provide both the necessary creativity as well as checks and balances against shifts that are not necessarily supported by objectivity as the basis for changes. The inability of almost 16 per cent of officers to perceive a coherent strategy also highlights the need for reassessing the policy of not coming up with defence, military and army strategies, either for restricted use or as open-source documents.

As India's role and responsibilities are redefined in accordance with its growing economy and influence, there is likely to be a demand for greater transparency and openness on these issues. Therefore, the government and the army must seriously consider coming up with its strategy or at least a doctrine periodically and preferably in the open domain. This will not only help create awareness, but also provide the much needed debate and inputs on issues of security, which remains limited as part of national discourse. This can best be accomplished with a simultaneous attempt by the government to outline a national security strategy, which becomes the basis for other strategies to be formulated.

PME forms an important constituent in the overall development of officers in the army. It arms the officer cadre with both theoretical and practical knowledge, especially on the basis of case studies. It also provides the foundation for understanding the concepts and practical realities for change management.

The question related to the adequacy of PME received responses which serve as an important input for military change (see Chart 5). While 29 per cent found it adequate, 50 per cent saw it as inadequate. Even amongst the "others" category, descriptions given by respondents were related more

Chart 4: Characteristics of Army's Strategy

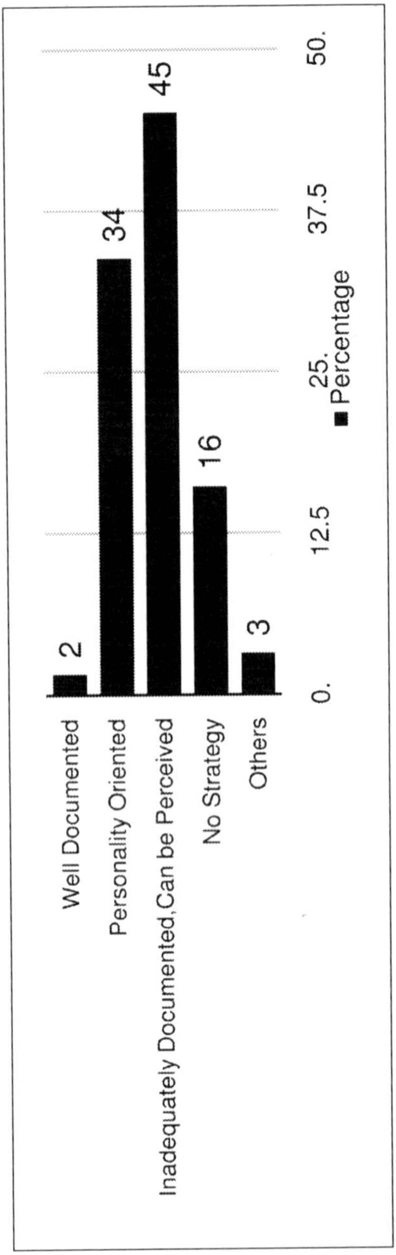

Chart 5: Adequacy of PME

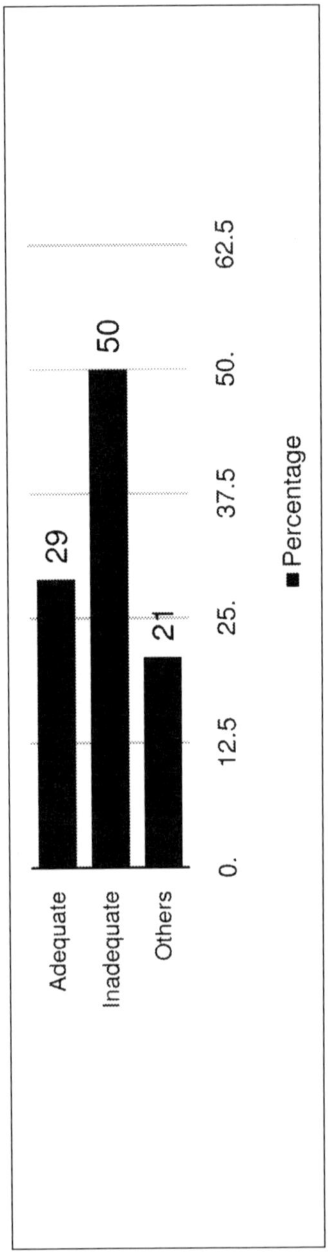

to the inadequacy of PME in the army, though described in their own way. This factor was further elaborated through a number of follow-up questions, in order to better understand the limitations of PME in the army.

The next question related to encouragement of innovation in the army. 87 per cent felt that it did not encourage innovation, while only 2 per cent saw it as giving a fillip to the same. Even amongst the 12 per cent in "others" category, the descriptions provided further elaborated upon the inadequacy of the system (see Chart 6).

In a similar question, attempting to relate PME to the ability to generate new ideas, 92 per cent felt that the educational system had failed to achieve it (see Chart 7).

Some of these issues were addressed by the next input, which dealt with the methodology of PME, in terms of emphasis on application vis-à-vis rote learning. 80 per cent felt that it was based on rote learning, while only 16 per cent saw it as related to application (see Chart 8).

The successful evolution of the officer cadre is often related to time spent on self-development and PME, and inadequate time is generally considered an impediment to good PME. Interestingly, the responses to the question relating time and other factors to PME threw up a contrarian view, wherein 66 per cent of the officers felt that it was not the limitation of time but an inadequate method of instruction that was responsible for poor PME. On the other hand only 14 per cent saw it as a result of paucity of time (see Chart 9).

The importance of relating PME to the case studies system of education was reinforced through the next question (see Chart 10). 50 per cent felt that there is inadequate emphasis on case studies, while 34 per cent felt that even as the emphasis was adequate, it was constrained by non-availability.

The quality of PME is also impacted by access to declassified material. The next question related to this factor. 47 per cent felt that material was hardly declassified, while 30 per cent felt that there was inadequate access to declassified material and 19 per cent said that they had adequate access to declassified material (see Chart 11).

Chart 6: Encouragement of Innovation by PME

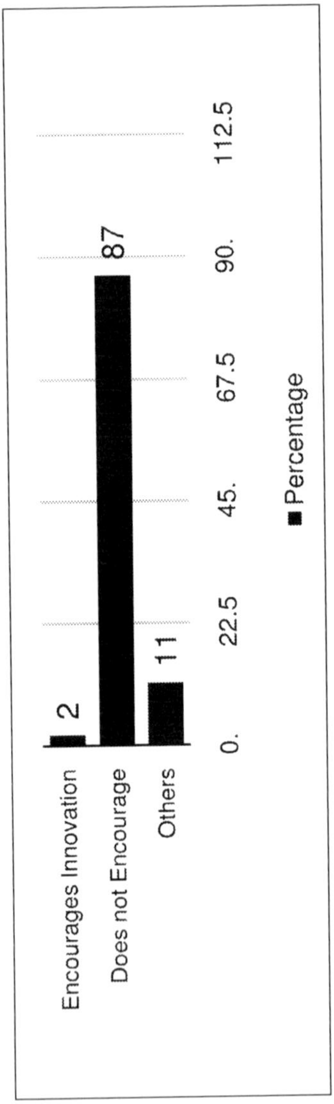

Chart 7: Does PME Generate New Ideas

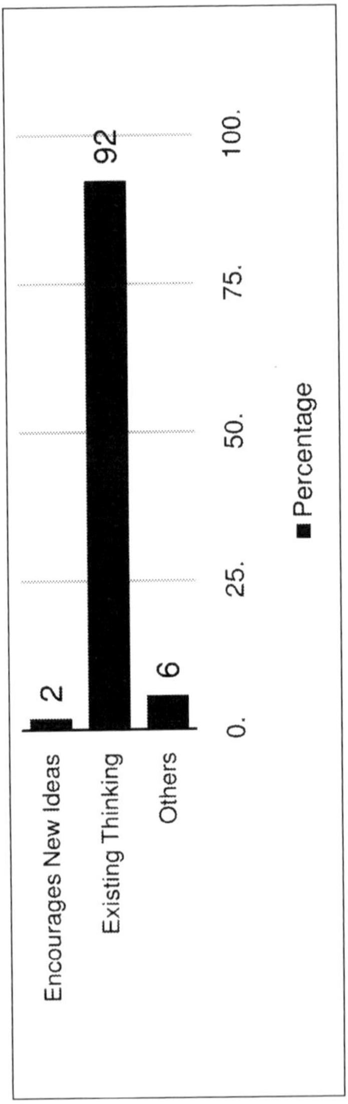

Chart 8: Employment of Rote Learning in PME

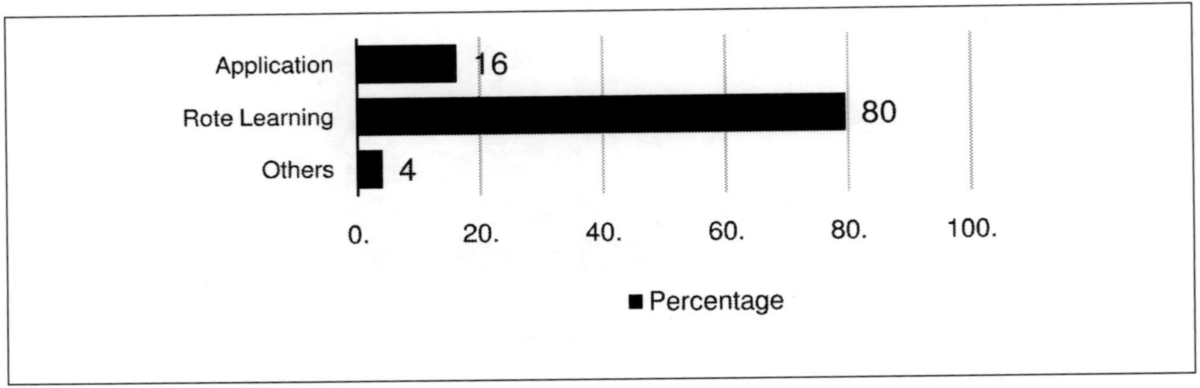

Chart 9: Factors Affecting PME

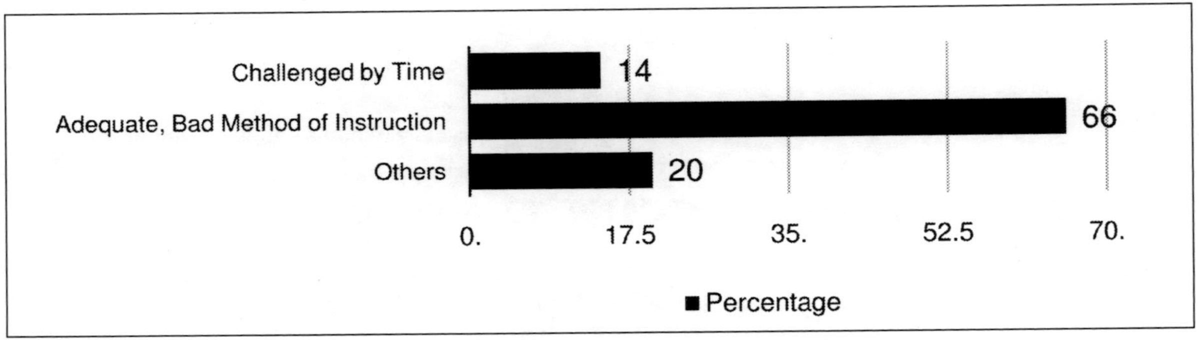

Chart 10: Impact of Case Studies on PME

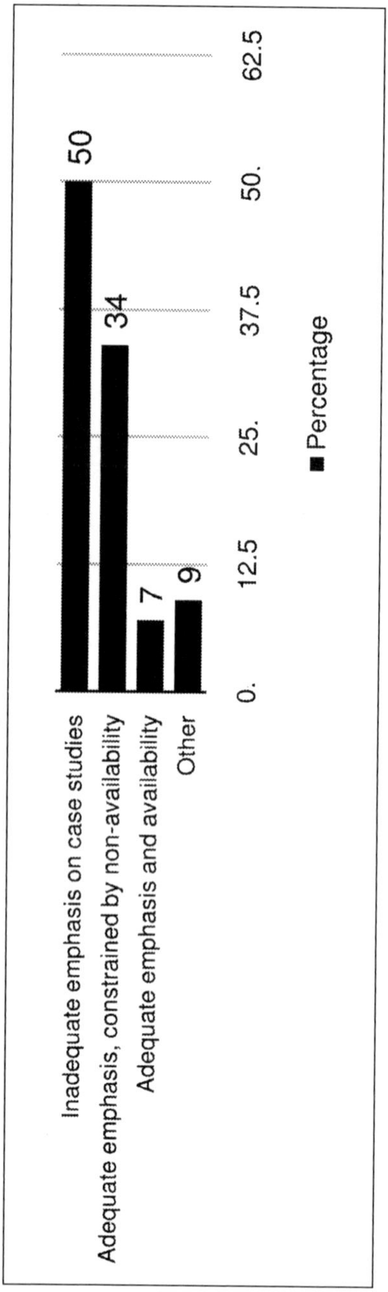

Chart 11: Access to Declassified Material in PME

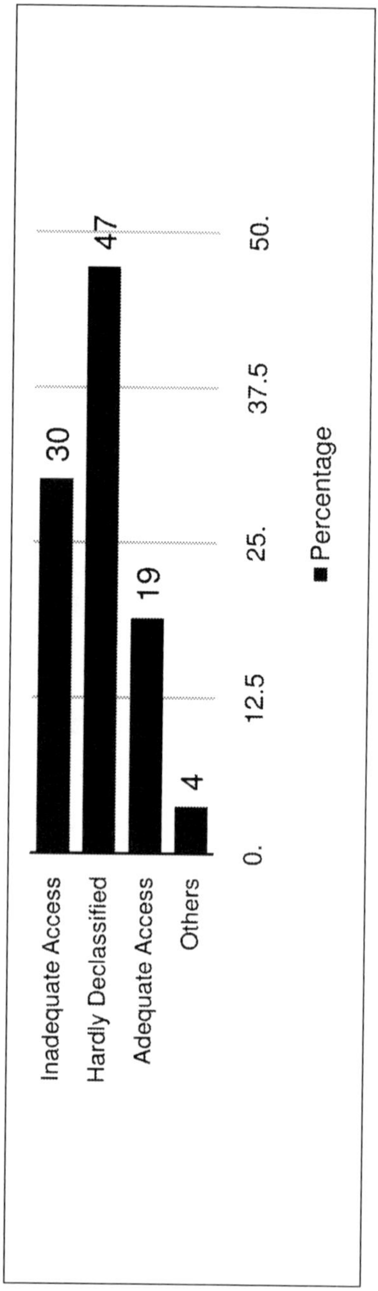

The questions related to PME were considered an important set of queries, since the professionalism of the officer cadre, their ability to learn from past mistakes and evolve as thinking soldiers are related to it. In turn, the issue of innovation and practical application of education further has a bearing on the ability of leaders and an organisation to adapt to change. The inputs received quite clearly suggest that the officer cadre remains deeply dissatisfied with the educational system in the army. It also indicates its inadequacy in grooming officers to achieve the level of excellence desired to best undertake their responsibilities. This becomes all the more apparent in senior ranks, where the sudden shift from the tactical to strategic domain requires a thorough professional understanding of warfare.

The next set of questions related to the reasons for successful adaptation at tactical level and the perception of inadequacy at the strategic level. The respondents had the option of selecting more than one reason in both cases. 57 per cent and 59 per cent of respondents felt that good junior leadership and experience of combat, especially in counterinsurgency (CI) operations were the most important contributors to tactical adaptation. In addition, 51 per cent related it to the adaptation under tough conditions, 38 per cent saw it as a part of regimental soldiering and 32 per cent as a do or die situation in a sub-unit, amongst other reasons (see Chart 12).

Further, 59 and 57 per cent indicated limited understanding of strategic issues and a weak institutional tradition or strategic culture as the reason for failure to innovate at the strategic level. 54 per cent officers felt that the system threw up the wrong leaders, 52 per cent that officers are dissuaded from strategic thinking in junior ranks and 50 per cent indicated that officers spent very few years in senior ranks which inhibits strategic thinking as also the lack of necessary exposure. 48 per cent linked it to lack of exposure and 46 per cent to the lack of incentive to take risk (see Chart 13).

The answers to these two sets of questions clearly reinforce the assessment that emerged from the case studies. It is evident that the tactical prowess of the army and the faith that the officer cadre has in leadership at that level is not evident at the strategic level. This is further highlighted when seen in context of questions related to strategy formulation, strategic culture and PME.

An important factor that is related to innovation at the strategic level is the limited time spent on professional development of officers. The next

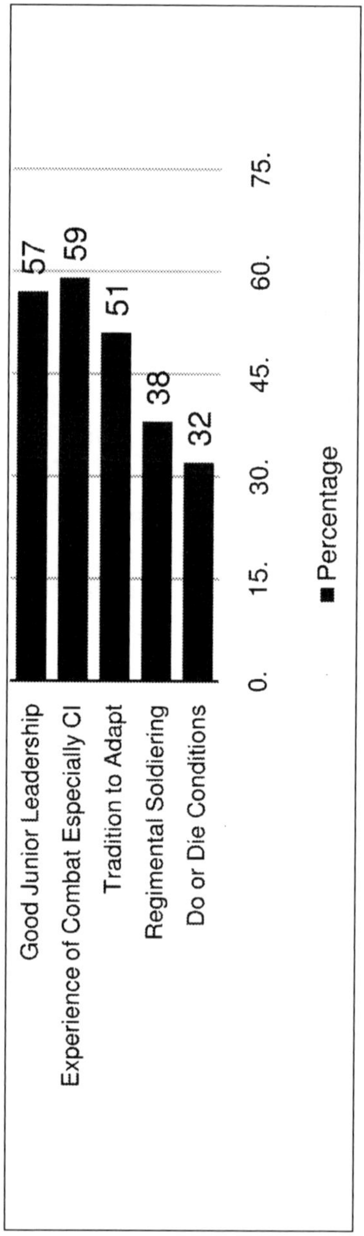

Chart 12: Successful Adaptation at Tactical Level

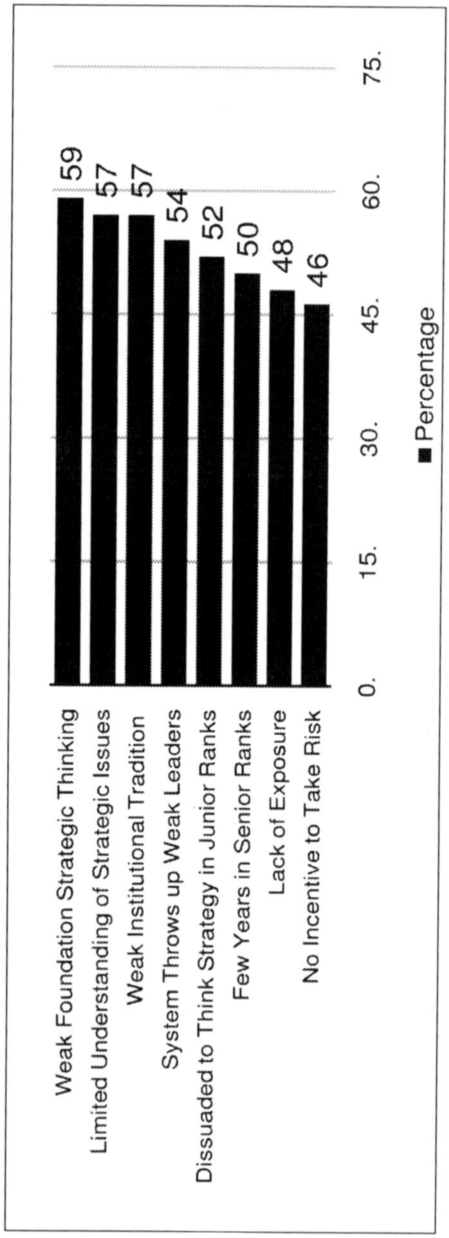

Chart 13: Challenges to Innovation at Strategic Level

question aimed to quantify the time give to professional development of officers. Of the total time available, 29 per cent officers believed 20-30 per cent time was being spent on their professional development, 27 per cent saw it as 10-20 per cent, 15 per cent as 30-40 per cent, 15 per cent as 40-50 per cent and 10 per cent as less than 10 per cent (see Chart 14).

Chart 14: Percentage of Time Spent on Professional Development

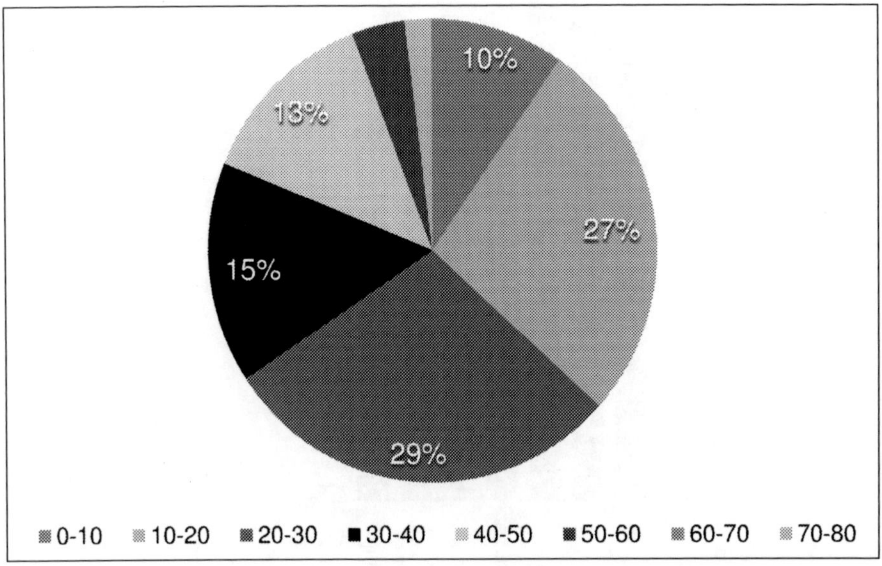

Further, the officers were asked to provide reasons for their inability to spend adequate time on professional development. This included the option to select more than one reason as the basis of this limitation. 72 per cent saw this as a result of the zero error syndrome that afflicts the army, which results in overdoing simple and mandated tasks. 70 per cent gave the reason as far too many formation-level commitments, which tend to be time consuming. 61 per cent attributed it to the failure to decentralise command and control, 50 per cent to stress on ceremonials and poor availability of officers for the responsibilities at hand, 41 per cent to bad time management and 39 per cent to routine administration (see Chart 15).

These two factors of time spent on professional development and its availability clearly illustrate the priority of the army and the adverse impact it seems to be having on the officer cadre. They evidently impact the officers' professional development, and lead to increasing stress on status

Chart 15: Factors Affecting Time Availability

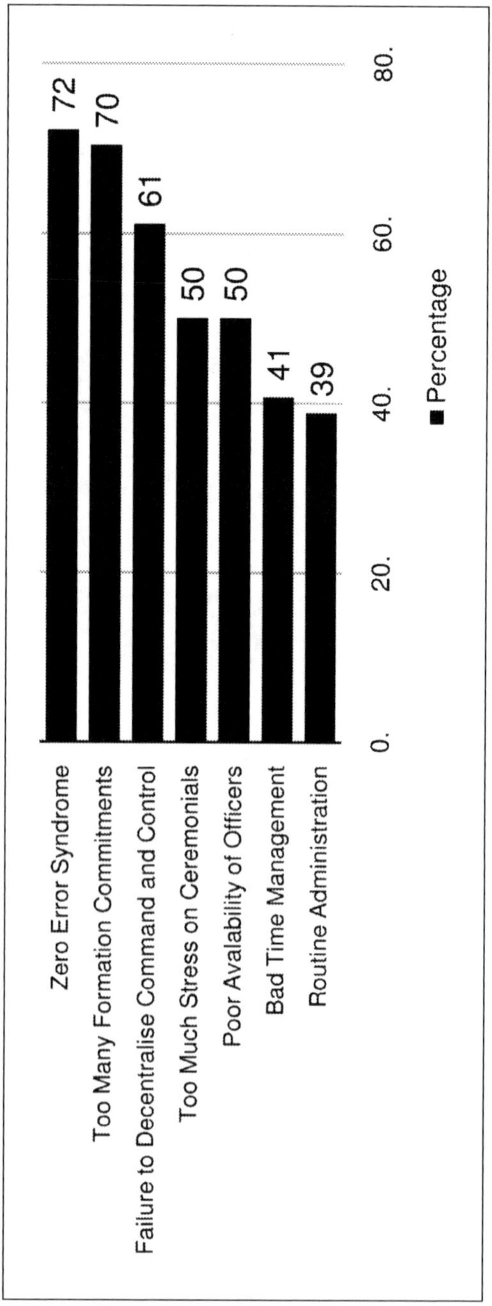

quo, which can be managed within the constraints highlighted above. These factors are also a reflection of the army's organisational culture, which in turn affects its strategic culture and professionalism of officers. Factors like zero error syndrome, time-consuming commitments and the failure to decentralise all point towards a hierarchical organisation, which will fail to encourage innovation and creativity. This is further impacted by shortages of officers in junior ranks, thereby constraining professionalism of the officer cadre. It must be noted here that the ability of junior officers to adapt in a CI environment is a testimony to their will and perseverance. However, systemic weaknesses seem to have a more detrimental impact, as officers progress in service.

The specific aspects related to the challenges to change management were addressed after highlighting some of its inherent prerequisites (respondents could pick more than one option). 69 per cent saw the main challenge as the lack of strategic perspective, 63 per cent as rigid hierarchy, 50 per cent as the inability to take risk, 43 per cent as the failure to effectively execute changes, 41 per cent as short tenures of officers and 30 per cent as the lack of political support (see Chart 16). The question reinforces some of the earlier inputs, which highlighted the inability to think big as a major constraint to change management, as also the environment in the organisation, which impeded change. Interestingly, the often highlighted factor of political support is further down the list, which quite clearly indicates that officers see systemic limitations to be more important constituents to successful change rather than political factors. This question also encapsulates in brief the highlight of the case studies and limitations noted therein. From weak strategic direction at the senior political and military level, to opportunities and a conducive environment at the junior level, change management faces an uphill task under these conditions.

The next question related change to its pathways and source (respondents could pick more than one option). 49 per cent respondents clearly indicated that while the military changes was based on Western concepts, it was adapted to local conditions. 37 per cent felt that it was influenced by Western literature and thought (see Chart 17). This clearly highlighted the pathway as primarily emulation and evolution, with limited emphasis on revolution, thereby reinforcing the assessment based on case studies.

Chart 16: Challenges to Change Management

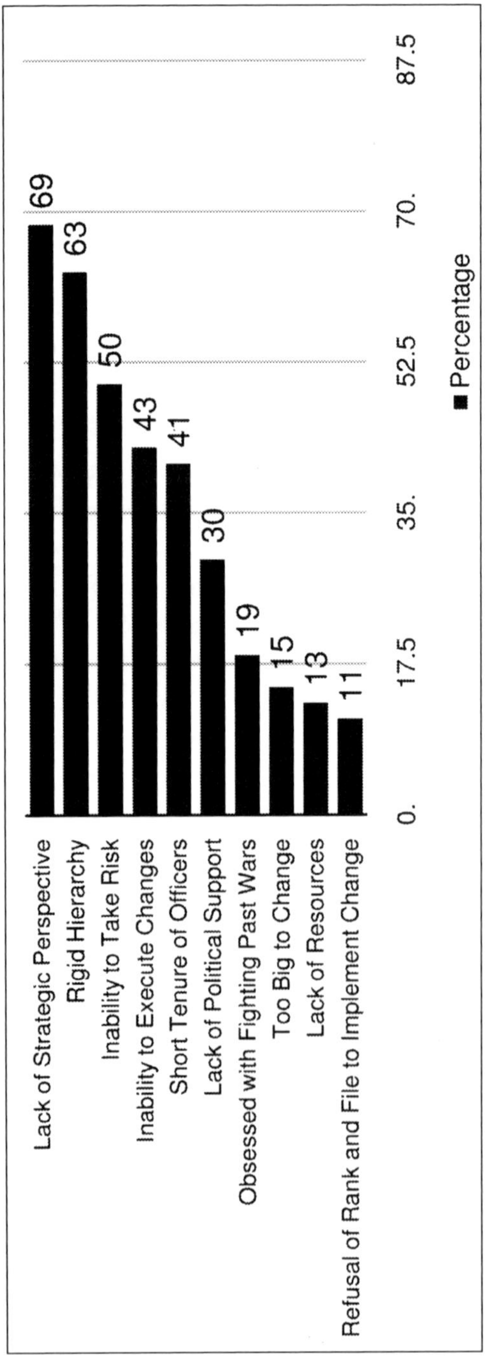

Chart 17: Source of Military Change

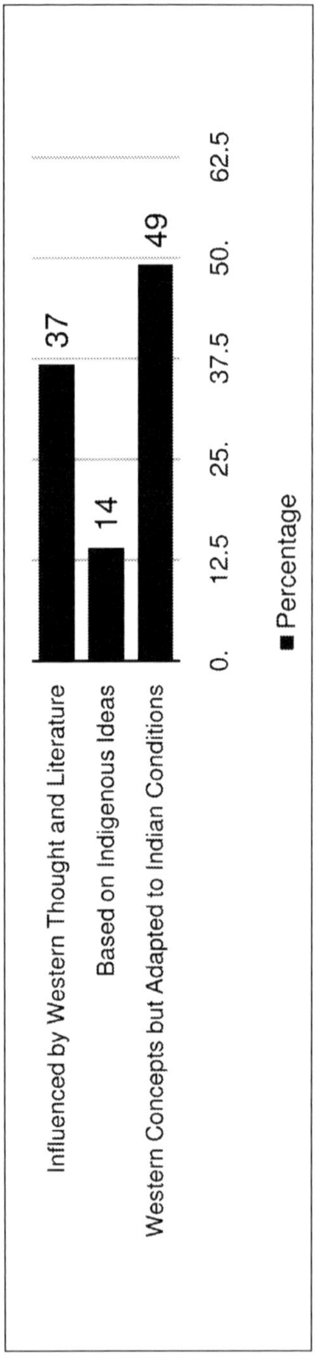

The last question related to the effectiveness of newly created organisations (respondents could pick more than one option) on the basis of a number of likely factors. 72 per cent officers linked the effectiveness to the adverse impact of weak direction, 63 per cent to lack of specialisation, 56 per cent to lack of clear mandate, 52 per cent to competing interests between organisations, 48 per cent to short tenure of officers and 39 per cent to poor institutional capacity. This is an important factor in relation to funding of organisations. A mere 15 per cent felt that limitations of funding impacted the effectiveness of organisations (see Chart 18).

This survey might seem, to some, a laundry list of problems highlighted by the respondents. However, it reinforces the previous assessment that as part of change, even if organisational structures are created, it remains a challenge to make them truly functional and effective in the manner that they were envisaged. Further, military effectiveness is adversely impacted by the organisation's inability to provide direction, staff suitably trained officers and give them time and continuity to ensure that they can deliver on the vision of leaders.

For any major change to be implemented successfully, the army must look beyond its comfort zone. The onus of absorbing change lies with the rank and file. The army's past record suggests that it has done so without hesitation. Therefore, it is the senior hierarchy, which must do the intellectual heavy lifting to provide the fundamental underpinnings for major organisational changes.

Every system has its distinct characteristics. The Indian Army, and for that matter, the armed forces are no exception to this reality. Therefore, they can innovate and change only to an extent and not beyond. The case of some other armed forces in the past suggests that this can best be resolved through political participation and direction, especially when related to organisational restructuring.

The changes post-1975 began with the mandate to improve the teeth-to-tail ratio of the army and reduce its strength. The report proved that effectiveness need not become captive to a larger force. The prevailing circumstances indicate that while change is imperative, it must break from the past instances of increase in manpower and budgets, if effectiveness has to be achieved. Perforce, this must flow from a modern force, which is derived from lower outlays for revenue expenditure, rather than demands

Chart 18: What is the Effectiveness of Organisations Affected By

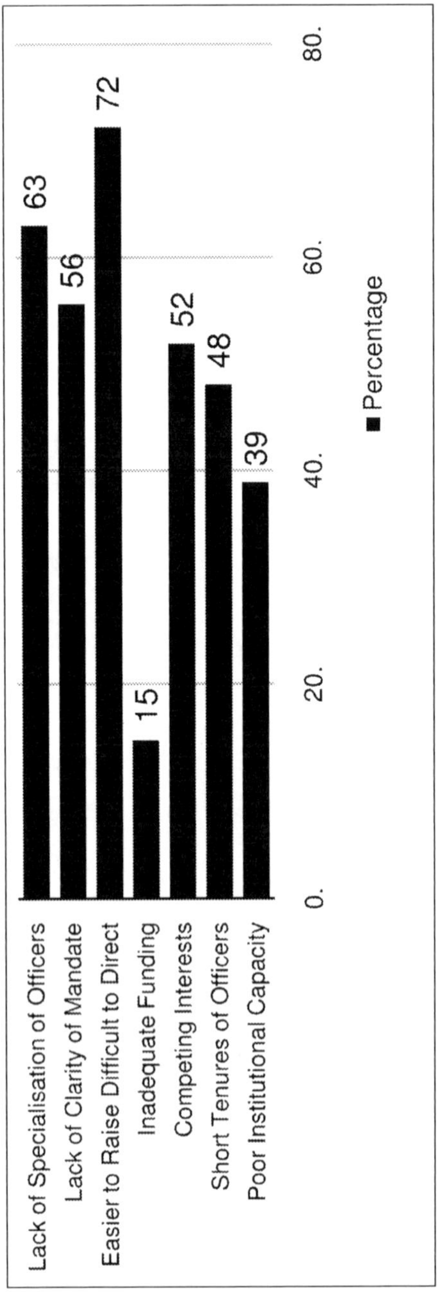

for increased budgets, which is unlikely to be met given other competing priorities.

Military change cannot happen merely because the army demands or needs it. It also requires a strong commitment of the political elite to support such change, and ideally with the army as a partner in the process. And this process must commence with a clear enunciation of national objectives to enable the army to plan based on a definite end state. For example, the debate over Cold Start could have possibly witnessed a very different culmination had the same been a tri-services initiative, duly backed by the government.

The book has made certain recommendations at the policy level, both based on the case studies and the larger context of the existing national security architecture in the country. This is followed by the results of a detailed survey which gives a very clear understanding of existing limitations and the areas which need to be worked upon by the army. A summary of these indicates two clear areas of emphasis. The first relates to the need to improve the learning culture of the army, which must strengthen the system of PME. It is a common refrain in the army that it suffers from being overtrained. This is possibly true as well. This raises questions regarding the nature of training being imparted and the impact it is making in its intended domain. Second, the army has not been found wanting in terms of creating new organisational structures. The limitation has been in making them deliver the intended output. Since a large number of these structures represent domain expertise beyond the immediate professional understanding of soldiers, especially in the sphere of information technology and warfare, the existing limited emphasis on specialisation will fail to derive desired results.

Change often flows from new ideas, which may be simple but represent a shift from "normal". The army's everyday adaptation in the face of adversity in CI operations is the best example of the need for flexibility and openness. Military change must therefore encourage, adopt and vigorously profess the same openness in higher institutions that drive policy, rather than being mired in red tape, a constant refrain that the uniformed community has against their fellow bureaucrats.

NOTES

1. Based on inputs from Lt Gen. H.S. Lidder, former Chief of the Integrated Defence Staff, during an interaction on May 20, 2016.

ANNEXURES

ANNEXURE 1

Illustration of Military Change in Counterinsurgency (CI) Operations

Sr. No.	*Case*	*Type of Change*	*Approach to Change*		*Nature of Change*	*Driver* *Impact*
1	Frontier warfare (1909-1947)	Strategic (military)	Top-down	Major	Operational threat	Change in military operational strategy
2	CI operations (1950s-early 1960s)	Strategic (politico-military)	Top-down	Major	Operational threat	Development of initial CI strategy of search and clear
3	CI operations (late 1960s-early 1990s)	Strategic (military)	Top-down	Major	• Operational threat • Environmental pressure (shaper)	• Development of clear-and-hold strategy • Discard protected villages strategy
4	Iron Fist Velvet Glove (Mid 1990s-2007)	Strategic (military)	Top-down	Major	• Operational threat • Environmental pressure (shaper)	• Creation of sub-conventional doctrine • Greater emphasis on humane operations
5	Major increase in force levels	Strategic (military)	Top-down	Major	Operational threat	Control over violence and peace in areas
6	Amendment in Legal Provisions (1997)	Strategic (politico-military)	Top-down	Limited	Environmental pressure	Reduced human rights violations
7	LoC Fence (2004)	• Operational • Strategic (Military)	Top-down	Major	• Operational threat • Technology (shaper)	Reduced infiltration (appreciably)
8	Local militia (1975 onwards)	Strategic (politico-military)	Top-down	Major	Operational threat	Helped resettle former militants Faulty implementation affected image
9	Use of offensive air support (1966)	Strategic (military)	Top-down	Major	Operational threat	• Limited gains • Alienation of population
10	Changing goals (1997 & 1989)	Strategic (politico-military)	Top-down	Major	Political directive Operational threat	Left military playing catch-up change Inability to achieve strategic objectives
11	Electronic warfare (1987 onwards)	• Operational • Strategic (military)	Top-down	Major	Technology	• Reduced own casualties • Facilitated precision operations
12	RR battalions (1991 onwards)	• Strategic • Organisational	Top-down	Major	Operational threat	• Continuity in area resulted in improved intelligence • Organisational structure suited for CI

(*Contd.*)

Sr. No.	*Case*	*Type of Change*	*Approach to Change*		*Nature of Change*	*Driver* *Impact*
13	Army Commanders Special Financial Powers (1997)	Organisational	Top-down	Major	Operational threat	Faster induction of equipment
14	I Battalion (1968-1970)	Organisational	Top-down	Limited	Operational threat	Improved capability of units in CI operations
15	Additional rifle company in battalions	Organisational	Bottom-up	Limited	Operational threat	Better coverage of operational area
16	Commando platoon	Organisational	Bottom-up	Limited	Operational threat	Better operational effectiveness
17	Establishment of training schools (1970)	Operational	Top-down	Major	Operational threat	Better understanding of threat
18	Night-vision devices (Mid 1990s)	Operational	Top-down	Major	Technology	Vastly improved operational efficiency
19	Creation and deployment of Ashi Pillai (1997-98)	Operational	Bottom-up	Limited	Technology (shaper)	Improved preparedness against IEDs
20	Readjustment of battalions	Operational	• Top-down • Bottom-up	Limited	Operational threat	Improved control over area
21	Strengthening and buffering of vehicles (1988)	Operational	Bottom-up	Limited	Operational threat	Improved protection against terrorist attacks
22	Local adaptive training	Operational	Bottom-up	Limited	Operational threat	Improved drills, procedures and capacities
23	Use of captured equipment (1988)	Operational	Bottom-up	Limited	Operational threat	Reduced own casualties
24	Modification of Rifles (1988)	Operational	Bottom-up	Limited	Operational threat	The modification was not very successful and had a minimal impact. However, subsequent induction of AK-47s gave a major fillip to the capability of infantry soldiers
25	Small team operations (mid 1990s)	Operational	Bottom-up	Limited	Operational threat	Reduced collateral damage and improved precision operations
26	Minimise collateral damage (Mid 1990s)	Operational	Bottom-up	Limited	Environmental pressure	Improved local support
27	Cordon and search discarded (Mid 1990s)	Operational	Bottom-up	Limited	• Operational threat • Environmental pressure (shaper)	• Reduced inconvenience to people • Replaced by precision operations

ANNEXURE 2

Region-wise Assessment of Military Change

Sr. No.	Case	Year/Time Period	Naga Insurgency (1955-till date)	Mizoram (1966-86)	Manipur (1964-till date)	Assam (ULFA) (1979-till date)	Punjab (1981-94)	Sri Lanka (1987-91)	J&K (1989-till date)	Remarks
1	Frontier warfare	1909-1947	NA	NA	NA	NA	NA	NA	NA	Afghanistan
2	CI operations I	1956-mid sixties		Yes	Yes	NA	NA	NA	NA	NA
3	CI operations II	Mid sixties-mid nineties		Yes	Yes	Yes	Yes	Yes	Yes	Yes
4	Iron Fist Velvet Glove	Mid nineties-2007	Yes	NA	Yes	Yes	NA	NA	Yes	Released formally in 2006
5	Use of offensive air support	1966 onwards	Support operations	Yes	No	No	No	Yes	No	
6	I Battalion	1968-1970	No	Yes	No	NA	NA	NA	NA	Three battalions converted for almost three years
7	Establishment of training schools	1970 onwards	Yes	Yes	Yes	Yes	No	No	Yes	
8	Local militia	1975 onwards	Rival groups	Yes	Rival groups	Yes	No	Yes	Yes	
9	Electronic warfare	1987 onwards	Yes	NA	Yes	Yes	NA	Yes	Yes	
10	Strengthening and buffering of vehicles	1987	Yes	No	Yes	Yes	Yes	Yes	Yes	
11	Use of captured equipment	1988	No	No	No	No	No	Yes	Yes	The Northeast had limited seizures of high-end weapons and equipment

(Contd.)

Sr. No.	*Case*	*Year/Time Period*	*Naga Insurgency (1955-till date)*	*Mizoram (1966-86)*	*Manipur (1964-till date)*	*Assam (ULFA) (1979-till date)*	*Punjab (1981-94)*	*Sri Lanka (1987-91)*	*J&K (1989-till date)*	*Remarks*
12	Modification of rifles	1988	No	No	No	No	No	Yes	No	
13	RR battalions	1991	No	No	No	No	No	No	Yes	
14	Night-vision devices	Mid nineties	Yes	NA	Yes	Yes	NA	NA	Yes	
15	Small team operations	Mid nineties	Yes	No	Yes	Yes	Yes	Yes	Yes	
16	Minimise collateral damage	Mid nineties	Yes	No	Yes	Yes	No	No	Yes	
17	Creation and deployment of Ashi Pillai	1997-98	Yes	NA	Yes	Yes	NA	NA	Yes	
18	Amendment in legal provisions	1997	Yes	NA	Yes	Yes	NA	NA	Yes	
19	Army Commanders Special Financial Powers	1997	Yes	NA	Yes	Yes	NA	NA	Yes	
20	Cordon and search discarded	Mid 2000	Yes	No	Yes	Yes	No	No	Yes	
21	LC Fence	2004	NA	NA	NA	NA	NA	NA	Yes	
22	Major increase in force levels	Different years	Yes	Yes	Yes	Yes	Yes	Yes	Yes	Accretion more based on building police strength and capacity
23	Changing goals	Different years	No	No	No	No	No	Yes - 1997		Yes - 1989

Sr. No.	Case	Year/Time Period	Naga Insurgency (1955-till date)	Mizoram (1966-86)	Manipur (1964-till date)	Assam (ULFA) (1979-till date)	Punjab (1981-94)	Sri Lanka (1987-91)	J&K (1989-till date)	Remarks
24	Additional rifle company in battalions	Different years	Yes	Yes	Yes	Yes	Yes	Yes	Yes	
25	Commando platoon	Different years	Yes	Yes	Yes	Yes	Yes	Yes	Yes	
26	Readjustment of battalions	Different years	Yes	Yes	Yes	Yes	Yes	Yes	Yes	
27	Local adaptive training	Continuous	Yes	Yes	Yes	Yes	Yes	Yes	Yes	

Index